A Private Sort of Life

A Private Sort
of Life

Bridget MacCaskill

Illustrations by Frances Pelly, RSA

Bridget MacCaskill

Whittles Publishing

Typeset by
Whittles Publishing Services

Published by
Whittles Publishing Limited,
Roseleigh House,
Latheronwheel,
Caithness, KW5 6DW,
Scotland, UK
www.whittlespublishing.com

© 2002 Bridget MacCaskill
illustrations © 2002 Frances Pelly

ISBN 1-870325-82-6

Printed by Bell & Bain Ltd., Glasgow

For Calum and Rory

and

Alice

Other books by Bridget MacCaskill:
(with Don MacCaskill)

Wild Endeavour
On the Swirl of the Tide
The Blood is Wild
Listen to the Trees (written with and for Don)

Content

Introduction

Otters are special! Once you have had the experience of watching them at play, foraging, eating prey on the rocks, or grooming, you tend to be 'hooked' and would like to know a great deal more of their way of life, where they are to be found and how they manage to survive. My late husband, Don, and I became interested many years ago and when he retired we planned and carried out an intensive study of the animal, a family unit of otters, on a then remote sea loch of the West Highlands. It involved long hours, and days, of patient watching, in all kinds of weather, stalking and examining their 'signs'. It was well worth it and that study, on a more reduced scale, has carried on to this day.

Based on the study, a film was made in 1988 by Central Television with Julian Pettifer and a book published in 1993 (Jonathon Cape) and republished in 2001 (Luath), both entitled *On the Swirl of the Tide*. But for a long time I have had in mind to attempt a more intimate account of the animal which would appeal to all lovers of wildlife and especially those who are unaware of what might be involved in the rearing of young cubs. It would be written in the form of a story by an unobserved observer! It would tell of the lives of two otter cubs, from birth until adulthood, their relationship with their parents and the other otter family on the loch, and their interaction with some of the other creatures there. Hence, *A Private Sort of Life*. Enter Kyle and Kelpie, Coll and Coire.

All the imagined events in this book are based on actual observation, either from watching the animals themselves or by interpretation of their signs – sprainting, foot prints, and so on. The scenes within the holt were, of course, not observed, but information for these was gleaned from Liz Laidler's excellent book *Otters in Britain* wherein she had access to tame animals.

These fascinating and delightful creatures, at the moment of writing, are doing reasonably well, occupying most suitable habitats on the coasts of these islands and even making a come-back into fresh water systems, now cleaned of pollution, from which they had long since vanished. They are survivors, but survivors must have the right conditions in which to exist. Though reasonably tolerant of human beings, otters need 'space'. Disturbance, often thoughtless and unintentional, by the rising number of people visiting the countryside and previously seldom-explored parts of the coast, could be a problem. Otters need quiet, secluded places in which to raise their families and the ever-increasing popularity of fishing, sailing and other intrusive water sports could mean a lack of suitable breeding holts. With possible global warming, too, that 'space' may be severely reduced – holts along river banks and lochs, both freshwater and sea, may simply disappear under rising water levels. Conversely, in other places, long-established waterways may dry up. We need to make provision for dealing with these problems as far as is possible, so that these animals can, indeed, survive. They are a valuable part of our wildlife and should remain so.

Bridget MacCaskill

An Important Event

A long narrow sea loch on a wild, west coast was cradled in gracious woods of oak, birch and pine. Higher still, on either side, conifer-clad hillsides climbed to sheer, fragmented cliffs and broken ridges. The shores were lined with ancient lava rock and at low water carpets of seaweed – green, orange and all shades of brown – spread seemingly endlessly to a faraway ocean. Small bays scalloped the rough coastline and were sheltered by heather-topped outcrops.

Beneath one such rugged bastion, hidden from inquisitive eyes, was the secret holt of the otter bitch, Kelpie. Cascading strands of ivy curtained its entrance, but soft moonlight filtered through to reveal the cracked and creviced rocks within. Tucked away in their furthest shadowed recess, on a bed of dead grass and leaf litter, lay two tiny cubs with their mother. Helpless and feebly kicking, they lay enfolded in the protective curve of her long, lean body – pale, grey, soft woolly fur against the warm seaweed brown of her own. Sound was the brisk rasping of her tongue as she cleaned them up, the soughing of the sea from far below the great rock, and the drip-drip-plop of falling water into a small pool outside.

At last, pleased with her effort, the mother lay back to rest and her offspring, toothless and mewing softly, blind but knowing a scent they must follow, began instinctively to seek her swollen nipples. Soon small mouths connected, small paws began urgently to knead and the rich, warm milk was generously flowing. To the soft surging of the sea and the trickle of waterfall sound outside was added the satisfied sucking and muffled grunting of the two small cubs. Coll and Coire had arrived safely in their otter world and had already begun their lifelong quest for survival.

Kelpie yawned, a wide-open gape revealing needle-sharp teeth. Weary after her labours, her head began to droop and heavy-lidded eyes to close. She glanced briefly at her family, still happily feeding, and gave another perfunctory licking to one of them. Stretching her long neck to scent for messages on the cold air which wafted into the holt, she found nothing to cause alarm. One more prodigious yawning, one jolting back into consciousness to make sure all was well, then, at last, lulled by the faint, familiar sounds of the night, she fell asleep. It was dark in the holt, the moon already passing it by. The otter lay peacefully dozing and her children suckled greedily, needing her life-giving milk.

Only a few moments later, a harsh scream shattered the silence. Instantly awake, Kelpie scrambled to her feet, rudely casting off her contented family, and with small ears erect, muzzle pointing to scent, waited to discover what else might occur or what might threaten her cubs. The call came again, unearthly, haunting, and seemingly from within the nearby birch wood. The bitch made no move but inclined her head further, the better to pick up the sound. In a moment, there came a reply to this resounding imperative, a caterwauling cry from much higher in the forest. A weird and awesome sound, pitched higher and wilder than the first, it reverberated over the treetops and faded away to the high cliffs above. At once reassured, Kelpie relaxed. Those were the raucous voices of a pair of foxes she knew. They often hunted the shore together looking for titbits in the seaweed. Somewhere up there on the rocky slopes of the hillside, the vixen had her den and probably young cubs to suckle. She had called an urgent message to her mate: *I am hungry*, and he had replied: *I am coming*. Even now, he might be padding softly and silently through the wood, a rabbit held firmly in his jaws. The otter bitch lay back and her cubs soon found her teats again.

At this first feeding Coire and Coll were soon satisfied. In a few minutes, their questing mouths were letting go and they lay quiescent, unresisting, whilst their mother licked milk-streaked cheeks and chins, and bottoms to stimulate the first faeces to come. At last, pleased with her work, she settled around her family once more, and they, eyes tight-closed and small chests rising and falling in a steady rhythm, immediately fell sound asleep. The mother slept, too, but she would wake at once should any danger threaten.

The moon, on its westward path, stole from the holt to the placid loch beyond. The cavern grew dark, its sides vanishing in the gloom, all detail blurred. A faint breeze whispered in the wood. A tawny owl, brooding her young, kee-wicked a sharp message to her mate: *I am hungry*. Responding from an old fence post close-by, he hooted a mournful reply: *I have nothing*, then took off to hunt over a hillside clearing. A wood mouse, hearing the soft swish of his wings, scuttled as fast as she could to her moss-lined nest beneath some nearby tree roots. The otter heard her pass but knew the sound to be of no consequence. The tide was climbing higher on the giant rocks of her home, eternally slapping their sides, smoothing and sculpting them into new sizes and shapes. Reassured by accustomed sound, Kelpie, content, snoozed as her cubs lay sleeping.

Beside the otter's rocky home and to the east of it, a small bay sparkled in the moonlight. Birch and ancient oak trees bordered its shore protecting it from southerly gales, and a buttress rock on its far side, as impressive as Kelpie's own, sheltered it from bitter east winds. Its waters were nearly always calm and, at low water, a scattering of rocks, clothed in seaweed the colour of an otter's coat, was spread as far as an otter cub's eyes could see. It was a great place for youngsters once they were old enough to follow their mother down to the loch. Here, enchanting little pools left behind by the tide would tempt them to discover the scent and touch of sea water. Here, they would learn to forage in the weed for crab, eel pout and other small items. Wild otter games would be played in the shallows and over the surrounding slippery rocks, gradually building confidence to further extend their exploring. Here, they could safely be left whilst the otter bitch foraged for the food which growing cubs seemed always to need. Here she would encourage them into the sea, first to frolic in the shallows, then to swim and then to dive, and finally, to follow her into the deeper waters of the loch to hunt for larger prey. Otter Cub Bay was an ideal haven, quiet and secret, and much-used by generations of otter families.

As the otter bitch rested with her cubs, it seemed that nothing could disturb or worry her. She could hear the muffled rustlings of deer in the woods close-by as they sought shelter for the night. They were of no concern to her and with the first light of dawn she knew they would be setting off again, restless as ever and searching for the early browsing of the day. A slight breeze rustled in the birches on the hillside, bending branches still bare of leaves. Down in the bay, the tide sang a customary song, washing idly over the rocks, stroking the tangle, parting its glistening strands, smoothing them back into place as it drew back for the next advance.

But then, suddenly, there was another sound, faint at first but gradually becoming more distinct. Kelpie stiffened. What was that? Once again, she was sniffing the tiny currents of air which drifted through the entrance to her holt. Once more, she was listening hard. A fox passing by in the heather outside? No. There was no scent of it and no swishing of spiky branches brushed aside. More deer treading softly through the bracken of the nearby clearing? No. Their feet would crumble the brittle stalks, a sound clearly heard by a sharp-eared otter. Surely, it was movement in the water and from somewhere in the bay below. A seal from the local colony? No, they did their hunting by day and usually hauled out on the nearby skerries for the night. She would often hear their gruntings and groanings as they shifted their great bodies to more comfortable positions on the rocks.

It came again, that tiny ululation in the water, more a pulse in the rhythm of the tide than any other definable sound. It reached the questing ears of the otter and, at last, she knew its cause. Had she been able to see it, a glistening v-shaped ripple was spreading wide over the water in the bay and a broad head was parting its surface. An otter! It came slowly, forepaws and hind paws dog-paddling along, a streamlined tail drifting lazily from side to side, matching the sinuous movement of the long, sleek body. It was Kyle, her mate. The dominant dog otter of the range was on patrol and checking for intruders in his territory. He whickered a soft greeting to Kelpie: *I am here*. And, comforted, she lay back with her family.

The moon had marked a silvered path across the bay but the big otter hugged the dark shadows close to the shore. He swam almost silently, scarcely causing a chuckle in the water through which he passed, and only Kelpie could hear him. He cruised slowly in and out of the rocks and weed, all the while checking the air for scent. A forest of seaweed waved tendrils to tickle his stomach. Sensing shallow water beneath, he rose on sturdy hindlegs and balancing tail to have a better look all around. But there was nothing to alarm. Taking a quick gulp of air, he dived into the tangle again and, with a flick of his tail and a kick with his hindlegs, rode ashore on a ripple.

The spray from his coat flew high as he shook it out, the droplets sparkling in a shaft from the moon. He examined the nearby rocks for spraint, sniffing the weed, parting the rubbery stalks to check, but found no evidence of an intruder's presence. Leaving a dropping of his own on a large boulder, a message both to his mate and to all other otters: *I have been here*, he took to the water once more. A few minutes later he was nearing the fortress rocks where Kelpie lay with her family. It was a nice, calm night and nothing untoward had happened. He was hungry and soon he would make for the deeper waters of the loch to hunt for a salmon or maybe a shoal of mackerel to chase.

Kyle reached the great rock outcrop and paddled slowly along its fissured base. He nosed into each shadowed crevice to test for the recent presence of an otter, but found no sign to indicate one. Further along, he climbed the rough sides of a large boulder to its smooth, polished top. Here was a favourite place for otters to bring fish to tear and eat. But there were no bony remains of food now, nor fresh spraint: no sign of a stranger not long gone away. His short-sighted eyes searched high to the towering rocks above where moonlight was painting dark shadows over the bitch's home. It would be difficult to spot any creature lurking there and he saw nothing in that eerie dappling of light and shade. But his nose was more reliable. Suddenly, he picked it up. The unmistakable scent of an otter not too far away! It came filtering down from the heather at the top of the rock and it certainly was not Kelpie's.

An interloper! Immediately aroused, the big dog kicked for the nearby shore, glided over a bed of seaweed and hauled himself clumsily out of the water. Quickly shaking the moisture from his coat, he set off across the glistening tangle towards a place that he knew well. Slipping and stumbling over the weed, leaping whenever he could from one small rock to another, he soon arrived at the bottom of a tall, narrow cleft. Almost splitting the outcrop in two, right to its jagged top, it was a difficult route to take and treacherous with scree and loose rock. But it was the shortest and quickest. This was the way he must go.

Kyle paused a second to catch his breath and to quickly look around. There was nothing to see, but the scent was strong. He hurled himself at the steep ascent, knowing he must quickly reach the top. It was a tough assignment – no safe foothold on these smooth unbroken sides and only the broad scree in the centre up which an otter might climb. But with each long leap at this difficult climb, hindlegs working hard, forepaws scrabbling frantically to find scarce hold, he was sliding back twice as far. He tried a fast scramble over the rough surface, using his claws to steady himself, and that seemed to work so long as he kept going all the while. A landslide of pebbles was sliding away from beneath him and a miniature hailstorm hitting the sea below. He was quite unaware of the sound it made. At last, with a leap that nearly missed its target and sent him toppling to the bottom again, Kyle reached a broad ledge. He ran to its furthest edge and peered over. Sure enough, in the adjoining bay and on the rocks below, an otter was eating a large fish. Kyle noted a young male who had no business to be there!

For a second the big adult crouched quite still, watching his rival. Then with an angry whicker, a hiss and a growl, he hurtled down to attack. The youngster heard him coming, looked up startled from his succulent meal, whickered surprise and alarm, dropped the fish and in a flash was making for the sea. In a flurry of glistening seaweed and flying pebbles, he threw himself into the water and a fountain of spray flew high in a moonlit rainbow. Momentum took him yards from the shore and then he rocketed downwards, sensing safety in the seaweed forest below – dark and kindly cover there for a frightened youngster. Spurred on by his fear, he dodged in and out of the swaying stems and did not surface again until well out in the bay. Once there, he paused only long enough to check for an angry otter in hot pursuit, before gulping in air, as much as his lungs would hold, and diving once again. With forepaws held tight to his breast, hindlegs kicking hard and rudder tail thrashing, he swam fast through the dark waters for the open loch.

Kyle noted his passage in a stream of bubbles, but did not give chase. There was no need, for his message had been understood. He finished off the lumpsucker and then began a careful grooming of his coat, licking the thick fur, nibbling and scratching the itchy places and rolling in the seaweed to complete the task. He looked high to the place where Kelpie had her holt. He could scent her there, but she had not come to greet him. It must mean her cubs were born and he would not be welcome. Indeed, she would see him off in no uncertain fashion if he ventured too close. He launched himself into the little waves that were rolling ashore, swam lazily for the centre of the bay and turned on his back to float.

In the west, the moon was sinking behind a silhouette of dark islands but in the east the sky already had promise of dawn. He lay quietly there, rocking on the gentle swell, satisfied that all was well. Soon he would hunt for a meal, then continue the patrolling of this territory. The incoming tide would help him on his way.

At Home in the Holt

Time passed slowly in the otter bitch's holt, her whole attention centred on the welfare of her family. She fed them, cleaned them and kept them warm, wrapping her long body around them to keep away the cold. She slept a lot, too, thus building up strength for energetic days ahead. When hunger drove her to hunt in the nearby loch, she was absent for only a short time and never far away, sometimes returning unsatisfied, so concerned was she for the safety of her cubs. No spraints were left near the holt, for these would give away their presence to a predator, and when she set off to forage she used several different paths to the sea. But a small patch of soil just outside the holt was becoming bare and worn, the vegetation blackened by the salt water shaken from her coat.

Life was just a feeding and a sleeping business for the baby cubs – wake from sleep, suckle their mother's rich milk, have a dim awareness of her rough tongue rasping, smoothing, caressing every inch of their bodies, then a sinking back into oblivion. They were putting on weight, although still weak and wobbly, and their woollen coats were already turning a darker grey. Home was a comfortable place, warm and dry, their bed of dead grasses ruffled but still almost clean – Kelpie removed and ate their droppings as soon as they appeared. It was a safe place, familiar with mother scent and the honey-sweet smell of themselves. Yet it was dark, for they were blind, their eyes tightly closed. Shafts of silver from the moon, as she passed them by, meant nothing; nor were they aware of daylight, when it came, turning darkness to murky grey and dimly illuminating the rough, rock walls of their home. Night and day were one and the same.

One morning, when the cubs were about a month old, a strange thing happened. Hunger woke Coll and he immediately began to search for his mother. Mother smell? Milk smell? Neither seemed to be present. He began squeaking, his hunger the more urgent as the minutes passed. The plaintive sound woke Coire and she, too, joined in the woeful chorus. Both cubs were calling, calling, increasingly frantic for a mother who was not there and did not respond to their need. They carried on for quite a while, moving restlessly about in the litter, lifting small muzzles to pick up her scent, and squeaking all the while. At last, tired out and unsatisfied, they sank down into their bed and were quiet. Their lullaby was a small breeze stirring in the nearby trees and the plop-plop rhythm of waterfall drops falling into the pool outside – sounds they could hear all the time and, therefore, did not really hear at all. Very soon, they nodded off again.

Suddenly, the familiar scent of their mother, close, strong and unmistakable, was drifting in from the entrance to the holt. Both cubs were wide-awake at once. They began squeaking with excitement, pointing eager noses to pick up her scent, certain of a good long feed to come. But, what was this? Where previously her arrival had been heralded by her scent becoming stronger and stronger and the sound of her shuffling body becoming noisier, it seemed instead as if a huge, dark something was there which was slowly moving towards them. Behind it, too, was another shape, pale and enormous. They stopped their calling, not as yet knowing fear, but surprised into instant silence. Then almost at once the first shape was looming almost upon them and, strangely, the pale shape behind it had vanished. They began to tremble with the fear of something unknown and tried to bury their heads in the litter. All of a sudden, awareness grew that the scent, so close, was a familiar one and surely their mother's. Then, it was all over. In the twinkling of an eye and with a reassuring purr, Kelpie was beside her family and settling down.

A significant moment had just occurred in the lives of the young cubs. When hunger was satisfied and the familiar cleaning-up operation again in progress, they once more noticed that strange, pale shape in the place from which their mother had come. It did not frighten them now, for she was right beside them and they were safe, but it did not go away. And, in the days to come, as they gradually became used to this curious opaque 'something' which could be large or small and sometimes not there at all, they noted mysterious dark shapes all around it and a connection between it and their mother's comings and goings. In the natural course of their growing, the cubs were discovering sight. Soon, those dark 'shapes' turned into the rough rock walls of their home and the pale expanse beyond a suggestion of another world from which Kelpie often appeared.

The orderly life in the holt continued – a feeding, a cleaning-up, and a sleeping, an absence of their mother followed by her expected return and its consequent satisfying meal. Feeble limbs were slowly strengthening, though the cubs still could not properly stand or walk. So they crawled around the small space of the den, exploring its every crack and corner, even wriggling a short way along that dark tunnel from which their mother always appeared. Then, those other-than-mother scents, which filtered into the holt, became more and more interesting. On a day, not so far off, an overwhelming need would tempt them to discover their source.

But first, there was a small lesson to be learned. One evening, just as dusk was merging into darkness and no bright moonlight pierced the entrance to the holt, Kelpie was curled snuggly around her sleeping cubs, happy except that she was beginning to feel the stirrings of a small hunger. She looked briefly at her family, replete and likely to be satisfied for a while, and thought of leaving them. Then, for some reason, she changed her mind. She had no idea why. Once again, she stretched her chin comfortably over the nearest cub and closed her eyes. She would wait for a while.

It was as well. All at once, still drowsy and content, the otter bitch's nose began to twitch. Instantly wide awake, she raised her head to scent. Muzzle pointing, ears listening hard, eyes straining in the darkness, she waited for a sign. Then it came. A faint snuffling and scraping at the entrance to her holt and with it a strange, strong scent full of threat to her cubs. Reaction was immediate. She struggled to her feet, rudely shaking them aside, then with coat ruffled, whiskers bristling and softly growling, she wriggled through the narrow tunnel as fast as she could. This rough awakening roused Coll and Coire to bewilderment and alarm. Instinct told them to remain silent and quite still, so they snuggled together for reassurance, poked their heads into the dead grass of their bed and never stirred. From the entrance to the holt came a loud hissing, angry growling, the sound of a heavy body charging and then, though it had no particular meaning for the cubs, the faint padding of a fleeing creature. Once more, the usual soft murmurings of the night could be heard. A little later, the rustling and shuffling of a large body, together with its familiar scent, heralded their mother returning to her family. Kelpie had just 'seen off' a large, black mink, a male, who had been busily investigating the scent near her holt. It had been a fierce encounter but the whole episode had only lasted seconds.

When she returned to her cubs, the otter bitch seemed twice her usual size – in fact, her fur was still standing on end and a most peculiar scent clung to her coat. It was a scent that they neither recognised nor liked. Kelpie, however, flopped down beside them as if nothing unusual had occurred and began a routine cleaning-up operation. That done to her satisfaction, and it did take a while to remove the horrible scent, she lay back, serene and comfortable, to rest. The cubs, finding everything back to normal, immediately forgot the episode, sought her teats and were soon happily feeding. Perhaps, though, a useful warning signal had unconsciously been taken on board. A certain, unpleasant scent had prompted instant reaction from their mother and a heated exchange with some other creature outside their home. So, all scent was not necessarily GOOD. That one had been BAD and should not be tolerated by their kind.

Coll and Coire were more active now, their small limbs growing stronger by the day. They could stand quite well without rolling over into helpless, wriggling bundles in the litter. Within the cramped confines of the holt they could play quite rough otter-cub games, nipping, kicking, boxing and squeaking loud protest whenever a bite went home. It was all low-key compared with the rough-and-tumbles they would soon be having in the big otter world outside the holt, but it was the beginning of the strengthening process which would equip them for survival. Their coats, though still woolly and soft, had become almost the same colour as their mother's, a beautiful rich brown that would go well with the seaweed on the shore. Their sight was improving all the while and scenting powers becoming stronger – tantalising scents finding their way into the holt must soon be investigated. They had huge appetites and their mother's rich milk no longer satisfied them. Constant demands for a feed and her teats growing sore from the constant biting of needle-sharp teeth, triggered the next significant step in the growing-up of her cubs.

One night, the bitch was away for longer than usual and the cubs were ravenous. They played desultory games with each other, paused to listen for her coming, heard nothing, dozed for a few minutes, then were restless again. Hunger gnawed in their bellies and they could not understand why the usual supply of milk was not available. Time dragged slowly by. They whimpered in their sleep, and were then wide awake again. The holt was dark and warm, the waterfall outside, beating its usual soft rhythm, the breeze in the birches whispering a soothing song, but they could not settle at all. They were hungry.

At long last, Kelpie's familiar scent was suddenly strong on the air. She was there! Immediately, they sprang to life and began the usual chorus, squeaking with excitement: *hurry, hurry, we are hungry.* Any moment, they were certain, she would be with them stretching her warm body on their bed, ready to give them a good long drink. But Kelpie did not come and there was no sign of her large presence at the end of the tunnel. They heard her call, a faint whickering sound: *come to me.* But this had never happened before and they were much too timid to obey. The call came again, full of invitation: *come, it is good to come, it is safe.*

The cubs became aware of another scent wafting in with their mother's. It was strong. It was different. It sent an urgent message to empty stomachs. They began squeaking again: *we are hungry, we are here, come.* But Kelpie still would not enter the holt, continuing those comforting sounds of encouragement. The enticing scent became irresistible. Suddenly, Coll began to crawl slowly, cautiously, along the narrow tunnel, hesitant and fearful, but all the while drawn by the interesting smell that seemed to promise food. Coire, tending always to copy her sibling in all things, fearful too but as hungry as he, was right behind.

The youngsters were only a foot or two into the passage, when both froze to the spot as one. That pale, shimmering space through which their mother often arrived when she returned to the holt, had become larger and brighter than ever and to eyes used only to the dark surroundings of the holt, it pulsated light in a truly frightening fashion. They tried to turn and flee, but could not – the tunnel was much too narrow. So they cowered as close to the ground as they could and waited for something dreadful to happen. But nothing did and in a moment or two both were anxiously testing the air once more. Mother scent was there, reassuring and inspiring confidence, and that other scent, compelling, inviting, was there, too. And, Kelpie was calling and calling. Ever so slowly, Coll edged forward, so nervous he was only dimly conscious of the rough rock and soil which scoured his belly. Coire, more cautious, waited to see what would happen. The light became stronger, the pale opening much larger, the scent overwhelming. Suddenly, both were scurrying for the entrance as fast as they could and, yes, their mother was reassuringly there, whickering a greeting and obviously pleased to see them.

The otter bitch had her paw over a strange, long object on the ground beside her; it was, in fact, a fine eel. Awkwardly with her nose, she nudged it towards the cubs and they scrambled to investigate. The scent was delicious. Their mother whickered encouragement, tore a piece from the still-squirming fish and ate it with evident satisfaction. But, though they sniffed at the beautifully odorous thing, exploring every inch of its slippery body, they could make no connection between it and the pangs from their empty stomachs. Kelpie tore another piece away, chewed it and swallowed it with obvious enjoyment: *this is good, try it.*

At last, the message was understood and perhaps hunger helped as well. Coll sank his teeth into the succulent flesh, found the taste good, and tried to tear a piece away. Alas, small baby teeth, though by now accompanied by newly arriving adult ones, could not cope. For Coire, too, it was the same. Kelpie came to the rescue. With her own fearsome molars, she tore a large chunk from the fish, munched for seconds, then dropped the whole mouthful in front of her cubs. The problem was solved. Greedily, they each grabbed a morsel, chewed briefly, then swallowed. Just what was needed. Immediately, they were clamouring for more and trying to seize pieces from their

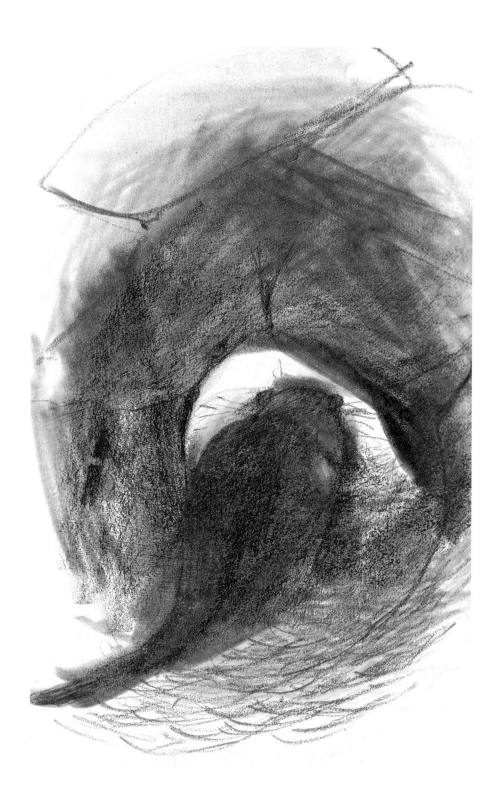

mother's mouth. She growled angrily, but the bothersome creatures, tails wagging furiously with the excitement of it all, chivvied her without mercy and squabbled over each mouthful of juicy paste. In no time at all, both small stomachs were full and tight, and both had hiccups! Kelpie quickly polished off the remainder of her fish then shooed her family back into the holt. They collapsed on to their litter bed and the mother stretched alongside. After a perfunctory cleaning, the cubs' eyes already closing, the whole family fell fast asleep.

A great step forward had been taken. The cubs, now about six weeks old, had ventured forth from their dark safe home for the first time and had tasted and found good the food upon which their survival would depend.

Home is Too Small

With that first juicy meal of succulent fish began a period full of new experiences and intensive learning for the young cubs. Their mother, until now seldom absent from the holt, was more frequently away hunting for her hungry, growing family. No longer was it necessary to encourage them out of the holt when she returned with fish. Whenever she arrived and made that enticing call: *come, I have fish*, they would wriggle out through its narrow entrance as fast as they could, squeaking excitedly, tails wagging furiously. In no time at all they would be greedily tearing its flesh and swallowing each mouthful as fast as possible. Competition was fierce and Coll usually came off better. With the addition of fish to their diet, stools became larger and firmer and Kelpie no longer ate them. Instead, she drove her infants out whenever they were about to drop a spraint – home must be kept as clean and dry as possible. They soon got the idea and this was another way in which they became used to the strange world outside.

The cubs were becoming much more active and the space within the holt was too small for the strenuous games they were beginning to play. With each visit outside for a meal sprouted a growing curiosity as to what lay beyond the rasping heather stalks and oddly shaped rocks and boulders which lay all around them. One morning, when Kelpie had gone fishing, they awoke from restless sleep and found themselves bored and needing to work off energy. They started one of their nipping, kicking and boxing matches, but, all at once, it seemed there was just not enough room. Coll broke away, gave himself a shake, yawned a mighty yawn, then sat looking around the jagged rock walls of his home wondering what to do next. He found himself staring at that familiar bright 'something' at the entrance to the holt. He thought of his mother and fish, but there was no sign of her return. An idea, entirely instinctive, was born. Why not go and see if she was coming? Why not see what was going on out there?

The young cub began squirming through the tunnel and Coire, bored as well and usually following her brother in all things, fell in behind. In only a few moments, they were at the entrance to the den and receiving their first surprise. It so happened that Kelpie had always brought them fish at dawn or dusk, a time when the light would be dim. Now they found themselves in a great blaze of brightness, the glare of the newly risen sun above the nearby forest. Used, as they were, to the gloomy darkness of their home, this was a frightening phenomenon and they almost turned to flee. But nothing alarming happened so they remained, cautiously sniffing a gentle breeze faintly redolent of their mother and fish and looking around them as far as short-sighted eyes could see. They noted tall shapes that were the trees surrounding their home, thick bushes of spiky heather and a patch of crisp, dead bracken with soft new fronds appearing. There were many different scents, as well, but none they recognised as threatening. Without their mother, it was all rather frightening, but they did not turn tail, just sat waiting to see what might happen.

In the silence that followed, the cubs became aware of the faint drip-drip-drip plops that were the familiar accompaniment to life in the holt. Now, they were much louder and, in addition, there was a pleasant tinkling, rippling sound as of something busily hurrying along but, yet, was a part of the whole. Tinkle, tinkle, plop, plop – a sweet melody with a regular beat that held them entranced. Curious, as ever, Coll took a step towards the remembered rhythm. The 'plops' became even louder and seemed to come from the middle of a wide expanse of something pale and strange right in front of him. It shimmered in the bright morning light in a fascinating way. And, after each tiny 'plop' a small circle spread out over this pale 'thing', then faded away into nothing. It was all very peculiar.

Come and see this, he called to his sister, and she, sensing his excitement, hurried to join him. Both cubs now lifted their noses to

scent this new phenomenon and found it strangely inviting. Noses to the ground, eyes fixed on this strange 'something' only a small distance away, they began crawling warily towards it. Nearer, and nearer they came. It seemed to be safe. Closer still. Then 'plop, plop'. A cool wet sensation hit each small forehead and trickled down each nose. Another one, and another. A drip-drip, and an itchy tickling 'something' running down each face to fall into whatever that funny 'thing' was beside them. The sound was an accustomed one, the sensation was not, but seeing no harm and intensely curious, the youngsters began poking their noses lower and lower, closer and closer, to sniff and test. Too low. Too close. There was a loud splash and both had fallen into what was, of course, the small, shallow pool beside their holt. The little waterfall above their heads chuckled merrily at their discomfort.

But otter cubs are born to spend a lot of their lives in water. Coll, once he'd got over his fright and found he was still alive, discovered this to be an exciting experience. He struggled to his feet and gave his coat a good shaking. A shower of droplets hit the pool all around him, then rippled away as wavelets to hit the shore. What was this? He slapped this strange object with one of his paws, a hefty slap for quite a small cub, and a fountain of spray, sparkling in the sunshine, flew every which way and fell in a flurry all around him. This was fun. He did it again. By this time, Coire, who was terrified by all the commotion, had scrambled and splashed her way to dry land. There, she shook out her coat, rolled in the bracken to dry it off, then looked to see what her brother was doing.

Come and play, the young dog whickered, *this is good*. So Coire, reassured, did just that. Very soon, the two were having the time of their lives in the pool, discovering quite by accident in the process, that they were entirely at ease in this new element. Rolling over and over in the shallow water, they wrestled, nipped, kicked, splashed, swallowed some water by mistake, and even started one of their energetic boxing matches. It was all great fun and soon they were whickering at the tops of their voices with excitement. But then, all at once, still being babes and not yet very strong, they found they were tired, all energy spent. The great game stopped as suddenly as it had started and they crawled, as one, out of this wonderful new 'thing'. After drying off their coats, they sat beside their holt as happy as young cubs could be, waiting for their mother – and food.

After this, the cubs treated the little pool, the heather and the bracken-topped outcrop of their home, as a normal place to be and a wonderful playground. Rough games of catch-me-if-you-can were frequent. The mother bitch often joined in, too, being nipped unmercifully on chin and chest, tumbled all over, wrestled with, and generally bullied, until, fed-up, she responded with growls and a snap of her formidable jaws. Then she would trot off into the heather for a little peace. Coll, already the larger and heavier of the cubs, was usually the leader, but Coire could hold her own. Often her brother received a vicious nip from behind which made him retaliate with an angry snarl. Then they tangled together in yet another fierce battle – defence and attack – a natural sequel to what had gone on in the holt and the means by which small bodies were filling out and limbs strengthening. Soft woolly coats, too, were thickening and becoming coarser and the waterproof undercoat, so essential to their survival, was growing in well.

The cubs began exploring the well-worn tracks, which led all over the top of the outcrop. Though each one smelled reassuringly of their mother, they did not venture, as yet, too far. The thick, stalk forest of heather branches, which was the predominant vegetation of their playground, could be tunnelled through, jumped over or hidden beneath as the game of the moment dictated. The nearby patch of crisp, dead bracken was a great place for drying off wet coats or a place to have a wrestling match. Large boulders, which were dotted all over the outcrop, often had mysterious holes and caverns beneath them and these were good hiding places in a game of hide and seek. Gradually, as they played their rough games and learned to follow the tracks of their mother, they were preparing – though they did not know it – for the time when they must fend for themselves in an otter world often harsh and challenging.

One day, the cubs encountered an enemy with whom they would often tangle in the future. A fierce game of tig was in progress, Coll tearing away from his sister through the spiky heather, up the bank and over the top of a monster moss-covered rock, and rocketing down again into the heather on the other side, and Coire, as usual, chasing gallantly after. All of a sudden, the little female found she was bored, had an itchy place on her chest which must be scratched, and remembered, while she was busy doing it, that the remains of their last meal was lying quite close to the holt. Instantly aware that her brother would guess what she was up to, she ran as fast as she could to be first. And Coll, of course, was immediately after her.

A terrifying thing happened just as they reached the deliciously smelly fish. A dark, silent shape, out of nowhere, passed low, right over their heads, squawking loudly and angrily. It swerved away and flew to a nearby tree. There it perched, on a gently swaying branch, regarding the cubs with calculating eyes that missed nothing. Both cubs, surprised and fearful, had instantly drawn back. What manner of creature was this? Nothing dreadful happened, however, so in a moment or two, with the fish still invitingly lying there, they moved forward to each seize a piece. Instantly, that same dark shape came swooping down: *qua-ark, qua-ark, that is mine*, it squawked. Coire, terrified, ran for the holt and disappeared inside. Coll stood his ground, instinctively knowing he might lose the fish to this creature and minded to keep a hold of it if he could. When the impudent bird came again, he growled fiercely and snarled, displaying a mouthful of needle-sharp teeth and ready to seize the creature if he could. Screeching furiously, the strange black 'thing' veered away, turned in a tight circle and came stooping again. This time Coll, all of a sudden not so brave, hastily drew back. The cheeky bird alighted beside the fish, lifted it in its talons and on hard-beating wings, for it was quite a large piece of eel, flew for the nearest tree. Perched precariously on a thin bouncing bough, it stared down at Coll for a moment, then took off and flew away with its prize to a nearby clearing. The young otter cubs had just met a large hooded crow and they would meet a great many more of these fearless predators in times to come.

One day, shortly after dawn, on a grey morning with a soft drizzle clothing the otters' home in glistening silk, the family was right in the middle of a rumbustious rough and tumble outside the holt. The cubs had just finished a good meal of lumpsucker and all three were whickering with excitement, enjoying the frolic, happy to play this game for ever. But then, all of a sudden, Kelpie broke away and would not play any more. The youngsters drew back puzzled, waiting to see what she would do. Something in the direction of the loch seemed to be holding her attention. Small ears pricked and nose raised to scent, she was listening hard and appeared to have forgotten their very existence.

It came again, faintly from the bay below, a call which lingered on the still air and was repeated. Then silence and only the sound of the sea lapping against the rocks below to break it. But, moments later, a scent, strong and unmistakeable, came wafting up from the bay and another call, too, loud and clear: *come, let's meet.* Without hesitation, the otter bitch set off along one of the much-padded paths that led to the sea. That call was from Kyle, her mate! As fast as an otter could, ignoring heather branches whipping her sides and dead bracken crackling beneath her hurrying feet, she began running for the shore. Arriving at the top of that rough rock gully, which was the quickest way down if she would risk its hazardous scree, she paused for only a second. Then, surprisingly agile for an animal more at home in the sea than on land, she hurtled down its steep sides, scrambling from one narrow ledge to another, clawing over smooth rock boulders with no safe purchase for her feet, sliding on the pebble-strewn surface and narrowly avoiding a headlong tumble to the bottom. Somehow reaching the shore, she scrambled on to a large, seaweed-clad rock. There, she lifted her nose to scent and pricked her ears for a message.

It came, another loud whickering summons from over the water: *I am here, come.* She replied at once: *I am coming,* then breasted into the welcoming water. Two otters now swam as fast as they could on a course that would surely end in a meeting. With seemingly perfect timing and with a common purpose in mind, each dived at one and the same moment and surfaced again only a few feet apart. Right in the centre of Otter Cub Bay, in swirling curtains of mist and water smooth and still, a great romping, rollicking greeting of otters took place. In ceaseless movement they curved and curled about each other, twisting and turning, kicking and nipping, rolling over and over in the glassy water, and all the while whickering at the tops of their voices – the sound echoed weirdly to the far side of the loch.

They drew apart, then Kelpie, gulping in a lungful of air and arching her back in a graceful dive, shot down to the seaweed forest below. There, they continued the splendid game, in and out of the waving stems, the bitch darting here, darting there, checking to see if her mate was following, but always just out of reach. The dog responded, matching her sinuous curving with his own, now this way, now that, swift and sure but never succeeding in giving her more than a playful nip.

At last, urgently needing air, both soared through the weed to meet on the surface. Their bond renewed, feet pointing skywards and tails twitching lazily from side to side, they floated on the gentle swell, resting after their tumultuous encounter. It had been a great otter get-together. Seconds later, as if nothing special had been happening, each rolled right-way-up and began to swim away. Kelpie had remembered her cubs and Kyle that he was on patrol and must check for intruders.

The Beginners

It was a dreich and dismal morning. Thick grey curtains of cloud in a leaden sky were sweeping across the loch, the long night lingering into day, reluctant to give way to light. Coll and Coire sat side by side at the entrance to their holt, hungry, miserable and calling for their mother. Wistful 'peeping' filtered through the nearby birches and would even be heard in the little bay beneath their home. Surely she would come.

But Kelpie did not come. She was there, all right, crouched in the heather some little way away and perfectly able to hear the pitiful cries of her family. For the moment, however, she was taking no notice and it was intentional. Her cubs must become so hungry that in sheer desperation they would come looking for her. Instinct had told her that it was time for them to discover a much bigger world than the small one around their birthing holt, one in which they must learn to fend for themselves and grow to be adults. A great adventure was about to happen for the young cubs.

Very soon, Coll and Coire grew tired of calling. They sat beside their home feeling neglected, the hunger pangs gnawing inside their small bodies, and totally at a loss what to do about this unhappy state of affairs. In a half-hearted manner, Coll began patting the water in their little pool, but was not inspired to start a game when the resultant splashes hit his face. So he sat himself down again to wait for a mother who would surely come – sometime. For a brief moment, his attention was caught by a small dark bird hopping from branch to branch in a tree on the edge of the clearing, but he had already learnt that he could not catch such creatures, so it was of little interest. Coire was snoozing nearby, in a favourite, comfortable coorie place in the bracken. He settled beside her, instead, then both were sleeping, the silence broken only by the whispering of a breeze in the nearby birch wood and the faint murmuring of the tide on the shore below. From time to time, they whimpered in their sleep because the hunger pangs did not go away.

At last, a call, loud and clear, came winging towards the hungry pair: *come to me, come.* It woke them, at once. Half-asleep, they sprang clumsily to their feet full of anticipation of the usual offering from a mother soon to arrive. Tails wagging wildly, noses scenting and ears, erect and sharp, pointing towards the path from which she usually arrived, they waited eagerly for her coming. Any moment now there would be fish.

But Kelpie did not come running to her cubs with prey. Instead, she called again and the message was clear, its sharp imperative an almost irresistible command: *come, I have food for you.* The cubs were frantic with excitement, prancing through their little pool in a deluge of dancing water, racing towards the heather trail, dashing back to the holt in a foment of anticipation of the meal soon to come. Once again, the otter bitch disappointed her family. Instead, as their squeaking died away in surprise and frustration, there was renewed silence, no further calling, and certainly no fish. The unending moments passed and it seemed a long, long time to the cubs. They waited, they wondered, they waited in vain. What was happening? Once more, their distraught 'peeping' filled the air and echoed far and wide over the surrounding hillsides – a vixen, hunting far above them in the forest, heard their hungry crying and remembered her own small family waiting for a meal.

Still no sign of Kelpie. Coll, both puzzled and increasingly desperate, decided to go and look for her and Coire, not wanting to be left behind, followed after. They trotted, quite confidently over the dead bracken clearing and on to one of their playground paths through the heather, certain that they would soon find their mother. Her scent was everywhere. There would, surely, be no problem. But then, almost imperceptibly, the bushy heather branches became thicker, taller, and tangled together overhead. No light flickered through to reassure them and the way ahead seemed dark, frightening and

full of hidden danger. Now, the track had become a sort of tunnel, gloomy, and with no ending in sight that an otter could see. Dismayed, they drew up. Wild games had never brought them to this place before. They checked again for their mother's scent, and it was there, all right, good and strong from one of her spraints. But they hesitated. This was new. This was frightening. Courage ran out and, as of one mind, they fled for home.

No sooner were the young cubs safely sitting outside the holt than they heard Kelpie call again and, desperate for the fish they knew she would have, they could bear the suspense no longer. She must be near. Headlong, they charged through the little pool, galloped as fast as short legs would permit over the bracken and, greatly daring, along the track through the heather tunnel. This time they continued further along, no harm having come to them before. But, once again, suddenly overcome by an overwhelming feeling that they were moving too far from home, the timid creatures came to a halt. They crouched in that frightening place, hesitating, wondering what they should do.

In fact, Kelpie was on her way to meet her family. Just as they were about to scamper back to the holt, they spotted her, a dim shape not too far away apparently at the end of the long, dark tunnel. She whickered a greeting and they tore towards her fully expecting to squabble over the fish she would certainly have. Another halt. Another surprise. There was no succulent meal on the ground at her feet. What is more when they began a half-hearted game in the narrow space, relieved to have found her at last, she rebuffed their overtures with a distinctly unfriendly growl. Coll sat down and wondered what all this was about. Coire followed his example. Both looked uneasily towards their mother to see what she would do.

Straightaway, the otter bitch turned right around on the track, knocking both cubs off balance into the heather, then whickered a soft invitation: *come on, follow me.* She trotted off along the path and instinctively they fell in behind. At first there were no problems. The route was well-trodden and easy to walk through. It held no terrors for the cubs and they hurried along, confident so long as they could keep their mother in sight. But then, just when they were getting used to this strange new experience, their surroundings changed again. Abrasive heather in the dimly lit passage became instead a steep, slippery bank, the ground all wet and soggy on a hillside in bright sunshine. The cubs blinked in the glaring light and paused in dismay. They felt horribly exposed, looked urgently to their mother for reassurance, but saw her still forging ahead. Soon she would be out of sight. What could they do? They dare not lose her again. They must follow.

Very soon, the youngsters were stepping cautiously, delicately, over an almost water-logged place where the vegetation grew thick and tall. It was a muddy trail, full of small puddles, and slippery to the unaccustomed feet of two young cubs. Twice they skidded off the track, rolling over and over down the slope until an opportune clump of ferns braked the fall and enabled a panicked scramble back up again. They came to a place where enormous boulders towered overhead and little rocks were littered everywhere. All were covered in thick, green moss, spongy and soaking like the moss that flourished all around their home. It washed their faces as they scurried past and was an encouraging, familiar sensation. They came to a giant rock and the path seemed to be right below. This was just like their holt at home and bothered them not at all; they crouched as low as they could and crawled right through to the other side. Water was everywhere, oozing out of the ground, trickling down the sides of the rocks, creating little rivulets which joined together to hurry on down the hill. They tried running to catch up with their mother, but this was a great mistake. Off balance, they somersaulted crazily down the bank, almost to the bottom, and, with difficulty, made their way up again. No matter what, Kelpie just trotted on ahead, regardless of any problems her family might encounter. She was in a hurry.

All at once, the cubs found themselves in yet another new place. Boggy ground had become firm and dry beneath their feet on short, well-cropped grass. There seemed to be no patches of heather or the crumbling bracken they were used to, instead there were trees like the ones which grew in the wood near their holt. Immediately, they felt more at home. Hesitantly, at first, their mother out of sight but her scent still strong, they set off to catch up with her. Confident, now, the track well-defined and obviously much-used, they padded along through the trees, winding in and out of the crusty stems, leaping over small branches which were scattered in their way. Then, once again, another surprise. There were no more trees. In their place, a seemingly endless patch of tall, slim leaves all shivering in the breeze and flowers on long stalks – iris. It was dotted all over with small oozing puddles. Another boggy area. Once more, they halted in dismay. Was this a safe place to go? They began 'peeping' for their mother, but she never came. In the end, they began, ever so cautiously, to step across.

At long last, they caught up with Kelpie. She was poised on the banks of a small burn and looking expectantly in their direction. When they rushed to greet her, however, she whickered in a friendly fashion but did not allow the usual energetic romp. She seemed to have some other purpose on her mind. So they sat close beside her, looking all around, and waiting to see what she would do next. This seemed a good place to be.

The little burn was chuckling merrily along beside the otter family, urging them on to another adventure: *come on, come on, this is the way to go*. It seemed to be hurrying somewhere very fast and was quite different to their little pool at home which did not go anywhere at all. There was a different scent on the air, too, vaguely familiar because it came with their mother to the holt, but all-pervading now as if there could be none other. It was tangy, sharp and exhilarating. As well, they noticed a strange, regular surging sound which was followed by a slapping, a rustling and a retreating 'swoosh' which faded away into a moment's silence – before beginning all over again. It was all very puzzling. After today they would recognise the smell of the sea and the sharp tang of the kelp, and know the sound of the waters of the loch as they lapped the shores of their little bay, Otter Cub Bay.

Kelpie had chosen a good moment for this new lesson. It was low water on a spring tide and the sea was calm – no great waves would come rolling in to frighten the young ones nor place them in danger of being washed away. A huge carpet of seaweed, all nobbly with the small rocks beneath it and full of interesting scents, stretched on either side as far as the eyes of small otters could see. It would be safe for them to explore should they be bold enough. Instinct told

Coll and Coire that this was just where they needed to be. So, when their mother began to lead them towards the sea, they dashed after her as fast as their short legs would permit. And, it quickly became a frightening business on this new and tricky terrain. On and on she went, sometimes leaping right over the rocks, sometimes clambering up, over and down the other side, and never once looking back to see if her family was safely behind. The cubs scrambled along as best they could, slipping and slithering over the treacherous weed, finding a way, somehow, around the craggy boulders when they were unable to follow over the top, but all the time instinctively driven to somehow keep up. They must not lose Kelpie wherever she might be going.

Then, relief. Great big boulders became, instead, a wide expanse of little pebbles and broken shells – pleasant to pad over – and soon merged with a soft carpet of sand all strewn with crisp tendrils of dead and dying tangle. The going became soft, their feet sinking in and making small puddles. All the while, the sharp tangy smell was becoming even stronger. Then... all at once ...they were there. A vast expanse of water stretched before them for ever into the distance, a very large 'pond', not a bit like the one near their holt. But they recognised water. Inquisitive noses were cautiously dipped in and the experience found good. But, then, another disconcerting surprise. That very same water was rippling away from them, sucking and sighing over the sand in a myriad tiny bubbles, then was lost in the large, frightening whole. But, no! Here it was again, hungry little waves sweeping towards them again, relentlessly coming to wash them away. It was too much. The cubs squeaked in alarm, turned around and retreated up the shore. They began 'peeping' for their mother.

There was no 'help' from Kelpie, however. Instead she whickered a reassuring message: *come on, this is good*, and ran straight into the sea to dive and disappear from sight. The cubs were terrified. No mother, no help, and no way would they enter that enormous 'pool'! But the otter bitch surfaced again quite close, ran back to her family, shaking a shower of salt water all over them as she came. She whickered encouragement then turned for the water once more. At last, instinct overcame fear. This was right. This was where they should be. Immediately, Coll and Coire were chasing after their mother to the water's edge. In a moment, without further hesitation, they were running into the shallows and splashing around like… demented otter cubs. The cubs had found the sea! Very soon, they were into one of their energetic romps, biting, boxing, rolling over and over in the comfortable water and swallowing quite a bit of it, too. And often, in the general excitement and quite unaware of what was happening, they lost their footing, fell over in a panic, and found themselves dog-paddling instead – thus, unconsciously, learning the first lessons in how to swim and stay afloat. Kelpie was there, as well, joining in the fun but also keeping an eye on her family in case of trouble.

In a little while, the youngsters grew tired and all this exercise had made them hungrier than ever. They began swimming alongside their mother and 'peeping' pathetically. So she brought them ashore and led them over to one of her favourite rocks. In fact it was a kind of sloping platform of rock, falling away towards the sea on one side, for easy access, but with a flat bit on the top all covered in weed – a nice safe place for otter cubs to be. Then she showed them what all proper otters should do when they came ashore, sniffing carefully all over the rock to see if any other otters, or predators who might be a threat to her family, had been there. Satisfied there had been no interlopers about, she deposited a spraint message of her own. Quite naturally, as if they instinctively knew what all this was about, the cubs followed suit.

This was just the beginning of a long learning process on the way to becoming adults able to take care of themselves. A great deal would come from copying the example of their mother, but, as they grew older, both good and bad experience would also teach them much. Just now they were learning that otters leave messages for other creatures – they didn't know why but that was evidently how it was, and this was how it would be with all the lessons that they would have to learn.

The next lesson to be learned was about how their coats must be kept in good order. The otter has a coat which is designed to keep its body dry and at a temperature that will allow it to survive in all kinds of weather and in all conditions in the water. The soft, fine fur

of the dense undercoat traps insulating air and is kept dry by an outer coat of long guard hairs which are well-oiled and waterproof. There is also a layer of blubber beneath the skin which gives further protection from the cold. By now, at almost three months, Coll and Coire had grown beautiful waterproof coats, although they were still fluffy and holding a lot of air. Kelpie now demonstrated what must be done.

She began by giving her own coat a thorough shaking, prolonging the action until her family cottoned on. Then all three were vigorously at work and showers of spray flew everywhere and fell in a deluge all around. The mother rubbed her neck and chest along the moist weed, rolled right over to wriggle and squirm her long body over its resilient fronds, ironing away the clinging droplets. The cubs thought this was great fun and followed suit, joyously kicking all four legs in the air to make their bodies do as hers was doing. So enthusiastically did they copy their parent that they kept sliding away, out of control, down the slippery rock to the shore, and had to scramble back up again. Finally, all three were energetically scratching their coats to ease spiky-looking fur back into place. At last, the family were all spruced up and ready to go.

But Coll and Coire were not going anywhere. Surprised and a little dismayed, they now received orders from their mother to stay just where they were. Satisfied they would obey, she trotted purposefully to the far end of the big rock, dropped another spraint: *this is my place, these are my cubs,* and clumsily, for she was in a hurry, slithered down its seaweed side to the shore. She ran over the tangle to the sea and without a backward glance at her cubs breasted straight into the little waves. A few yards out into the bay, she dived … and that was the last they saw of her.

The young otters, however, were quite used to their mother leaving them for a while, so they were not unduly disturbed by her sudden disappearance. Anyway, they were tired. In a moment or two, they curled together in a nice little hollow near the top of the rock and to a lullaby from the sea fell sound asleep. Being the same colour as the luxuriant weed all around and lying quite still, at least for a while, a passing predator would not easily discover their presence. But, of course, they were soon wide awake again and missing her. Panic set in. Where was she? Where had she gone? The shore stretched endlessly on either side of their rock and, what was this – that enormous 'pool' with its regular lapping rhythm seemed to have come much closer than it was before. They began to be very frightened. Loud 'peeping' filled the air and echoed all around the little bay and the cubs were quite certain that their mother must hear them and come. But she didn't come … and didn't come. After a while they gave up and there being nothing else to do, settled again to nap.

In fact, Kelpie was not away for long. Her dive had taken her out into a dense forest of seaweed only yards from the shore, and as she coasted past a gently swaying curtain of kelp, she spotted the give-away twitch of a tail. An eel! In a flash, a deadly torpedo was speeding unerringly towards its target, and the otter pounced. Eel saw otter too late and there was no escape. With an extra kick from powerful hind legs and a flick with broad tapering tail, the otter shot in, caught the slippery creature in her jaws, then rocketed for the surface. Safely there, she paddled hard for the shore as fast as the struggling fish would allow.

Coll and Coire sensed her coming and, immediately awake, looked towards the sea. And, there she was, a dark, familiar figure rising from the water and, without a doubt, with a fish in her jaws. As yet, they were too cautious to go to meet her, which was just as well. That fish was doing its best to escape and the otter bitch was having quite a job to hold it. Dragging the struggling creature over the rough, uneven shore, she would not have welcomed dubious help from her famished cubs. But, suddenly, the youngsters could bear the suspense no longer. Squeaking with excitement, they jumped down to the shore and began slipping and sliding over the treacherous weed, nipping each other when one or the other got ahead and already squabbling over who should arrive first to grab a bite. At one and the same moment, they reached their mother and at once tried to seize her fish. What was this? Kelpie growled fiercely, a low threatening sound which said: *get off, go away*. She dropped the fish, secured it with her paw, rested a moment, then continued up the shore, hauling the creature along with difficulty. Surprised and ravenous, the cubs hurried along to catch up.

At last, the otter bitch pulled her prey up the side of the big, flat-topped rock where the cubs had been sleeping. Here, they would be safe from the incoming tide. She dropped the eel on the tangle and a right royal battle began. Each cub fought fiercely for a share of the gleaming thing, growling, seizing, holding on not letting go, tearing with sharp teeth, and greedily swallowing as each mouthful was won. The otter bitch, also hungry, joined in the fray and their angry whickering could be heard all over the loch. Anyway, it was a large fish and, really, there was plenty. In a little while they were all eating peacefully together and in the end only a few discarded pieces of skin remained. A large gull, perched on a nearby rock, waited to polish off any scraps, but it was no threat to the cubs while their mother was there.

Satisfied now, stomachs comfortable, the whole family sat giving themselves a big cleaning-up, whiskers, cheeks, chests and anywhere else that needed it. Then Kelpie noted the tide rolling in ever closer and decided it was time to go home. She called to the cubs: *come, follow me,* sniffed to the far end of their rock, dropped a spraint, and that done, leapt down to the shore. Coll and Coire dutifully obeyed. Scrambling over the slippery seaweed, the tide at their heels, they all trotted quickly up the grassy track beside the burn, and soon disappeared into the gloom of giant rocks and tall, waving ferns. On a track that would now no longer hold fears for them, the cubs were on the way to their fortress rock. Soon they would all be curled together in a coorie place close to the holt and sleeping off a fine fat meal.

Learning to Live

The scent on the shore was wonderful – fishy and tempting if only the source could be found. Coll and Coire stood side by side on that spread of small pebbles where the little burn of yesterday joined the shore. It was as busy as ever, sparkling in the sunshine of a clear, sunny morning and hurrying to meet the sea. They had been playing near the holt when their mother called, seemingly from some distance away, and hungry as usual and perhaps with a faint memory of an exciting adventure, they had responded at once. Running as fast as short otter cub legs would allow along the heather path which led to the sea, they knew that a fine meal would be waiting for them. They could almost smell it!

But when they arrived beside the burn there was no meal and not a sign of their mother anywhere. As they looked around for her all-providing presence, the sheer immensity of this new, vast world of the seashore in which they found themselves alone, once again rang instinctive alarm bells. The carpet of shimmering seaweed appeared to pulsate with a life of its own and stretched as far as their eyes could see. The 'pool' of the day before, now restless and rippling in a turning tide, glinted in the sun with an alarming brightness that dazzled their eyes. And, for the first time, they noted the monster jumble of rocks at either end of the little bay – soon they would recognise one of them as their home, but now they looked alien and perhaps a threat to their safety. The cubs were not at all happy, but something prevented them from turning tail and running for the holt. For one thing, there was that familiar scent of their mother drifting on the air, now stronger, now weaker, so surely she must be somewhere near. In a strange way that they could not understand, the tang of the sea and the sound of the little waves washing the shore also made them feel that this was a place that was good and where they needed to be. All of a sudden, fears forgotten, they were feeling the urge to explore. But, where was Kelpie?

The otter bitch, in fact, was quite close to her timorous family. Midway between the end of the little burn and the sea there seemed to be a curious rock that was different to all the others. At one and the same moment, it caught the attention of both Coll and Coire. Covered in seaweed like nearly all the others, it was behaving in a very odd way, heaving up and down as though it was alive, rising slowly up then sinking quickly down again, pausing for a moment to be still, then moving on again. The cubs nearly fled for the safety of their holt but, instead, inquisitive as ever, crouched as low as they possibly could and waited to see what would happen.

All at once, there was a great upheaval in that curious 'hump' in the weed. It became agitated, rose higher and higher in its thick brown covering, and long strands of the tangle, glistening and dripping in the sunshine, began to fall apart over something strange and truly terrible. Rigid with fright, the cubs watched the head and shoulders of a strange, dark animal rising slowly out of the clinging tendrils and becoming more and more frightening with every second. Suddenly the whole of the creature was revealed and, they could not believe it – a very large otter was shaking itself vigorously and looking all around. It was, of course, Kelpie! Her offspring recognised her immediately and, though not quite brave enough to go running to her, started joyfully to call: *we are here, we are hungry, here, here.* But their mother ignored their urgent 'peeping' and, instead, whickered her own sharp message: *come, follow me.* Reassured and ravenous, sure she must have food at her feet, the young otters scampered over the rough uneven rocks as fast as they could, skidding on the slippery weed, stumbling on the little boulders in their way, and rolling over and over, out of control when to be first at the prize banished all caution.

They might have saved themselves the trouble. There was no tempting repast, no fish lying on the rock ready for them to squabble over. Instead, the otter mother demonstrated to her cubs what they must do if they wanted something to eat. Without further ado, she began to lead them over the treacherous weed, carefully sniffing here, sniffing there and seemingly looking for something special. From time to time, she busily scraped the thick strands aside but, apparently not finding what she was looking for, continued across the wide expanse. Each small rock was minutely examined, each crack and crevice explored by her enquiring nose. But still, she had no luck. The cubs tagged along, deeply interested because the smell of a meal was everywhere, but though industriously sniffing at the tangle themselves, they had no idea, really, what this was all about.

Of course, Kelpie knew exactly what she was doing. She had brought them to a place on the shore where there were large rocks dotted everywhere. All were clothed in seaweeds of different varieties, brown, green, orange and yellow, and most had small pools close beside them – perfect habitats, though the cubs did not know it, for all manner of sea creatures waiting for the tide to climb the shore again. Then, without warning, the otter bitch came to a halt beside a monster of a rock with a small pool beside it. She crouched low, absolutely still, and body language told her family to do likewise. Always obedient, Coll and Coire followed her example, their dark coats blending beautifully with the surrounding cover. What was going on? Their mother was evidently watching something in the pool. But what? With rising excitement, they waited to see what would happen.

Kelpie stood poised in total concentration, head slightly bent to one side, whiskers gently twitching, ears erect, nose urgently pointing. Suddenly, with lightening speed, her head shot down to cleave the water with a mighty splash, and then, as quickly, was up again. In her jaws she gripped something with wildly waving legs which she dropped, at once, and instantly pinned to the ground. There was immediate recognition. Food! Fish! Her offspring needed no further command. With excited chirruping and chattering, they rushed towards their mother anxious to be the first to grab. Coll, of course, arrived first. He darted in to seize a bite … and, for his pains, received a nip on his nose. A strange creature, this! He recoiled in surprise and with a startled hiss. Coire was more cautious. She watched her mother deftly turn it on to its back and not until then did the cubs receive an invitation to eat. The little female deftly avoided the flaying legs and nipper and quickly tore a morsel from the soft underparts. Her brother, not to be outdone, patted this new sort of meal with his paw and found it no longer aggressive. He, too, tore off a piece and ate with great satisfaction. But, that was that. It had been their first shore crab and a very small offering ... they were still hungry.

The young otters now understood that food was to be found hidden in the tangle and in the little pools scattered all over the shore. The scents all around them were inviting and they needed no further lessons. Now, three 'humps' were searching the shore, scenting, sniffing, and poking their heads into the shimmering strands to discover what lay beneath. All the time, the cubs kept a wary eye on their mother in case she found fresh prey for them. When she pounced again, however, and came up with a small fish, she ate it herself. Nothing for her family. The youngsters looked on dismayed but gradually the 'penny was dropping'; they must hunt for their own food. So when Coll disturbed a small eel in a tiny pool full of feathery weed, he made a clumsy sort of lunge for the creature, struck lucky and then managed to hold the slippery thing in his mouth. Before it could get away he had crunched and swallowed. Coire pounced on a shore crab, which was scuttling for shelter, and found she could control and eat it. The youngsters thought this was a great game and satisfying, too. Soon, both were catching the small creatures which were lurking in the weed till the tide returned to set them free. All were good to eat.

So Kelpie had shown her family one way in which to catch a meal, but she knew that it would take a great deal of successful searching in the weed to find enough to fill their ravenous stomachs. Now she would give her cubs perhaps the most important lesson of their lives. Now was the time to show them how she had caught that large eel of yesterday in the deeper waters of the bay. She called and her family reluctantly obeyed – hunting in the weed was fun. But so, for a while, was the next adventure. Tiny wavelets were rippling on to the shore, proclaiming to the sea urchins, razor fish, starfish, crabs, and the like, that the little rock pools in which they

had survived would soon be revived in the rising tide. To the cubs, the inviting prospect was irresistible. They forgot all about fish and remembered, instead, the fun of the day before. A great whickering and splashing began in the shallows and then all three were into the inevitable rough-and-tumble, turning the quiet waters of the little bay into a cauldron of boiling bubbles. The whole family was involved and the young ones had quite forgotten their earlier fears. This was all right. This was how it should be.

They would have played until exhaustion sent them running ashore, but Kelpie had only just started lessons for the day. Suddenly, in a moment when Coire surfaced to draw in a breath, she realised Kelpie was nowhere to be seen. At once, panic set in and she began a wistful calling for her mother which immediately alerted Coll. He came swimming quickly to join his sister, then both were frantically paddling round and round in the water, looking everywhere. Had she dived? Then she would reappear at any moment. She did not. Had she swum ashore? They could not see her anywhere. They lifted their voices to the heavens: *we are lost, where are you?*

Just as the cubs were about to make a dash for the shore, the safe place they knew of, Kelpie popped up right beside them. Joyous greetings were quickly suppressed. *Come on, this is what you have to do*, she seemed to say, and as she started swimming further out into the bay, the young otters, not wishing to lose her again, followed faithfully. At first there was nothing to alarm them, but then, as their mother continued on and on towards that wide open immensity of the open loch, they began to feel much deeper water surrounding them and realised that a mysterious world of which they had no knowledge lay beneath. No matter. Kelpie was there and surely they were safe.

But, all of a sudden, she was not there. The cubs noted her rise in the water, then with a curving of her body dive out of sight, down into that frightening place they could see below. By now, they recognised seaweed, the tangle which flourished on the shore and slowly swayed in the shallows, but this was quite different. Their mother had vanished into a dark forest of tall stems and feathery fronds which seemed to bow to a current strong and irresistible – a seaweed forest they would soon be at home in. Heads down, they could see her gliding around in the strange place, tail flicking gently, forelegs and hind working smoothly. She seemed to be searching for something. Then she was catapulting towards a dark cavern between two rocks. A moment later, miraculously, for once again they were afraid they had lost her, she came swimming back to them with a struggling eel in her jaws.

Fish! Food! Fears forgotten, the cubs dashed towards her, frantic for a meal but then recoiled in dismay. What was this? Growling fiercely: *this is mine, keep away*, Kelpie rolled over on to her back and proceeded to eat the delicious thing herself. The cubs were shattered. Paddling slowly round and round, 'peeping' pathetically, they watched the fish disappearing into their parent's busily chewing mouth. Then, once again, she uttered an imperious command: *come, follow me*, and dived down to begin hunting again. Coll and Coire could follow her every move, but were much too afraid to try and join her. They didn't know how, anyway.

Almost at once, impatient with her reluctant family, the adult returned: *come on, come on, it's safe, it's good*, she urged, then once more was streaming below. Coll, watching his mother cruising in and out of the restless stems, began to feel he would like to be there, too. He took a deep breath, placed his head right down into the water, gave a great kick with his hindlegs and a big scrabbling, paddling with his forelegs – and thought he must surely be getting there. This stupendous effort only used up all the breath in him, so he panicked. Up came his head to gasp and splutter and, surprise, surprise, he was still on the surface! He was no longer frightened, however, and instinct told him this was something he must do, so he kept on trying. Soon, when his mother rose out of the water to snatch a breath, he was able to follow her most of the way down. He didn't know it, of course, but his nostrils and ears were automatically closing when he dived and he quickly discovered that if he stopped working hard at the paddling, the air still trapped in his thick woolly coat would bring him rising to the surface.

Meanwhile Coire, panicked by the repeated disappearances of both mother and brother, had made for the shore and was 'peeping' miserably from the top of a rock. Kelpie, well out in the bay and keeping a watchful eye on the antics of her male cub, was suddenly aware of the sound. She paddled slowly towards her, calling all the time from the shallows: *come, it will be all right*, and the young female, not wanting to be alone any longer, splashed joyfully to meet her mother. They swam together, further and further from the shore, and Coll, now confident and playful, romped towards them. He was all for starting a game, but Kelpie warned him off. This was not the moment. She arched her back in an elegant dive and sailed down below, and he was happy to try and join her. Energetic attempts to dive were resumed.

In spite of all this encouragement Coire, who could see her mother swimming languidly in and out of the forest stems beneath her, still could not summon up courage to try to join her. She just coasted around in the nice safe water and, of course, lifting her voice to the heavens all the while. The otter bitch soon put the matter right. Sweeping close alongside her timid child, she grabbed her by the fur on her neck and took her, unresisting, speeding down below. Somewhere there, in the murky forest, she released the small creature to take care of herself. It was not a cruel action for she knew what would happen and, anyway, the little one had to learn. As had happened with her sibling, the young bitch panicked with the need for air. She instinctively kicked for the surface, and with the help of the air still trapped in her coat, arrived safely there. To her surprise, she found she was still alive!

The lesson was not yet over. Suddenly Kelpie was beside her once again, swimming slowly, smoothly, invitingly! This time, perhaps because Coire had found her recent plunge into the depths not too frightening after all, she seized a mouthful of the fur on her mother's neck, scrambled on to her back and holding tight, found herself speeding down to the bottom. Once more, cast off to fend for herself, she kicked hard for the surface and finding herself once more there, decided this was a good thing to do, after all. From that moment on both cubs were entirely happy in this exciting new element, practising diving skills, and romping as well, noisily whickering their enjoyment to the whole of their world. The otter bitch swam lazily up and down, keeping an eye on her family, always alert and ready for trouble.

Of course, all this exercise had made the cubs ravenous, and all the commotion in the water would mean that any fish sheltering among the rocks had long ago made for safer places. When they began to tire and to call for food, Kelpie knew she must hunt further out in the loch. She dived deep and long and, as far as her family was concerned, vanished from sight. They were getting used to this now so, finding themselves alone, they swam back to the shore and made their way over to that great big safe rock of the day before. There they did all the things that they had learned previously, drying off their coats with an energetic rolling in the tangle, scratching infant fur back into place with sharp claws, and finishing off with a huge shake. They even sniffed over the rock for scent and Coll left a spraint. Then they sat watching the intriguing shore all around and thinking more and more about food.

Kelpie did not keep them waiting too long. She had caught a large lumpsucker and was bringing it ashore when the cubs spotted her coming. With a tumultuous splashing in the shallow water and spray flying everywhere they tore towards her, each anxious to be the first to arrive. She dropped it on a rock close to the water, and while they squabbled over the red-bellied fish, returned to the sea to find prey for herself. Very soon, she could be seen rocking on her back in the gentle swell, enjoying a well-earned meal held in her paws, resting after her labours, but keeping an eye on her family all the while.

Deep Sea Diving

A brave little flotilla set forth across Otter Cub Bay, Kelpie leading the way with Coll and Coire, in strict line astern, as close as her energetically kicking hindlegs would permit. It was shortly after dawn and the early morning sun highlighted glittering quartz on the giant rocks of their home and threw its many cracks and crevices into shadowed relief. This had been their birthplace and where they had spent their early days. It would always be a refuge in need and a reassuring presence to be near, but now they were off on a great, new adventure and it would never again be the only safe place that they knew.

Instinct had told the otter bitch that it was time for her young family to know more of the range of Kyle, their father, Tangle, his other mate, together with her cubs, and the area in which they would lead at least the first part of their lives. The whole of the long narrow loch was their domain, with its rocky shores and wooded hillsides, its many small bays and rugged rock outcrops, and its burns which in rainy weather would come storming down the slopes in a flurry of foaming white water, to meet the loch. Today would be the first of many exciting experiences for the cubs as they gradually became acquainted with the world in which they must learn to survive.

Kelpie had decided to cross the loch with them, a long swim which would be quite a challenge. She had chosen a good moment. The tide had ebbed to its fullest extent and was slack, so they would not have to battle with a strong current. There was scarcely a breath of wind, so they would not receive a buffeting from a rough sea.

She would show them the best way for an otter to cover a long distance with as little energy as possible.

First of all, Kelpie kept swimming on the surface and Coll and Coire, following obediently, found the going easy. They had become quite strong swimmers, by now, and paddling hard they found no difficulty in keeping close to her, changing direction when she did, altering speed as required. Sheltered by the giant rocks at either end of the little bay, its surface was a mirror reflecting the bright dawn, and a long shaft from the just-risen sun cast a glittering gold path across the still waters, seeming to urge the youngsters onwards: *this is the way for you to go.* The great adventure had started well and the youngsters sailed along confidently enough, unafraid in their mother's presence.

But they never reached that golden way! All at once, just ahead of them, Kelpie was arching her body in a familiar action, putting her head down into the water, and then was, apparently, on one of her dives into the depths below. Nothing unusual in that. It happened all the time in the shallow waters of their home bay. The cubs were about to copy her example when, suddenly, the awful immensity of the huge loch dawned – it seemed to stretch for ever in front of them. Seemingly too, there was unfathomable water beneath their bodies and no kindly forest of the tangle there in which to hide or hunt. Their mother had disappeared. Where had she gone? They were terrified, and if the distance had not been so great they would have tried to swim for home.

However that golden path of sunshine was still ahead of them and there, miraculously, in only a little time, was Kelpie, bobbing to the surface in her usual way. She called: *I am here. Come. It is safe.* And the cubs, having no choice really, began swimming to join her. They sped towards her, whickering their joy, and she allowed them to nuzzle into her sides for reassurance. Almost immediately, though, she was diving again into that mysterious world below and if they did not want to lose her, they must follow. And, there she was! A dim shape, not too far away, powering on down, down, down into a dark and frightening place. With hindlegs together, kicking as strongly as they could, each rudder tail thrashing up and down, and forelegs held tight against their breasts, the cubs chased after her.

Seconds later, Coll and Coire found themselves in a mysterious world that they had never experienced before and, once again, they panicked. Small lungs felt as though they were bursting, energy was fast running out and they were very, very frightened. Kelpie must have known this for, in a moment, she had changed direction and was kicking for the surface, her frantic cubs right behind. When, at last, they arrived there she gave them a short break, encouraging them to nose in close to her floating body, resting them, letting them gain confidence from her calm, matter-of-fact behaviour. If they had thought about it at all, they would have noted that the golden path from the sun, which had seemed so inviting and to ever beckon them onwards, was no longer there. They never did find it for they had passed right underneath!

The little group was well on its way now. Beyond the shelter of Otter Cub Bay they had become more exposed to a light westerly wind and that, too, was quite a useful lesson for the cubs. It brought little waves to slap against their faces when they swam on the surface and though their mother's large body sheltered them a little from this new assault and their nostrils seemed automatically to close as the water overwhelmed them, it was necessary to rise higher in the water to safely take on the air they needed for the next dive. Down below, it was smoother and easier swimming in a world that was relatively still and had no little waves. In fact, it was the best way to go and required the least effort.

All the time, there were new and strange things happening. Small objects floated past on a current which was, of course, the rising tide building in strength. Dead vegetation, plastic bottles, bits of wood, and all sorts of things they quickly understood to be harmless and not edible, slipped by without threat. Other strange phenomena were more alarming. On one of their dives, for instance, when they were swimming nicely along behind their mother, a pulsating wall of sparkling objects appeared out of nowhere in the waters ahead. A great curtain of perpetually moving objects, brightly lit above and shadowy below, was streaking here and darting there, sweeping up towards the light above or swooping down into the depths below, and all the time surging relentlessly towards them. The cubs were alarmed and would have broken from their parent to make for the surface. But, suddenly, just when it appeared that they must be overwhelmed, the whirling mass split down the middle, passed on either side of them and then, as one again, spiralled away into the darkness. This was their first meeting with a shoal of herring.

This startling experience caused Coll and Coire to shoot to the surface and, safely afloat in the gently rocking waves, they swam frantically round and round searching for their mother. One moment she had been beside them, facing this fearful 'enemy', the next she

was no longer there. They were lost, something dreadful would happen. But, once again, just when they were becoming desperate, Kelpie popped up from below and not far away. In her jaws, silvery and shining, she was gripping a large fish. Food! Restored immediately, the youngsters, whickering with relief, shot towards her. She turned away, growling fiercely: *this is not for you*. Disappointed and hungry, they kept a respectful distance whilst she calmly devoured her prize. The adult had caught a herring as the shoal was passing and, thereby, had shown the young cubs another source of food to be hunted and caught: fish to be found far out in the deeper waters of the loch.

The last juicy piece demolished, the otter bitch dived again and the cubs, disappointed not to receive a meal, followed after her. And this was how it continued for what seemed, to them, a very long time – a gulping in of air, diving and swimming, a shooting to the surface for a short swim and more air, then diving once again. It seemed an unending journey, their overwhelming priority to keep as close to their mother as possible.

Coll was going strongly, for he was a fine, well-grown cub by now. He found he could swim quite well in this enormous 'pond' which seemed to have no end and when his mother took them hurtling down into the depths, where there were no cheeky wavelets to buffet them, it just needed an extra hard kick and a flick with his tail, to go soaring back up again for the next gulp of fresh air. Quite unfazed by this new experience, for this was obviously what otters had to do, his fear began to vanish. Coire, on the other hand, was beginning to tire. Smaller and, as ever, more timid than her brother, although she could swim and dive as well as he, she was becoming exhausted. This great adventure was surely going on forever and would never end. There was no friendly forest of seaweed down below in which to hide from danger and no bottom scattered with rocks to explore for a meal. Indeed, there seemed to be no bottom at all. As the long moments passed and the endless journey continued, she became more and more fearful. Now, whenever they broke through the wavelets, she began 'peeping' pathetically: *I am frightened, help me.*

In a little while, Kelpie responded. Turning full circle, she swam alongside her panicking daughter, sank beneath her small body and, rising, took the ailing creature on to her back. Then Coire was sailing along merrily, the chubby waves smacking her face but causing her no problems, her only need to hang on, for dear life, to her mother's thick coat. Coll, of course, thought this was a great idea. He began chivvying his mother to take him on board, as well, and, needless to say, was repulsed with a growl that could only have one meaning: *get lost*! In the end, he gave up. So they continued onwards, a large otter with a curious hump on its back and a smaller one in its shadow determined not to be left behind.

If the cubs had noticed how far they had come, they surely would

have been scared, for the shore they knew so well and the buttress rocks on either side of their little bay had long since disappeared into a hazy distance. Perhaps Kelpie realised, as well, that she needed to bring her tiring family safely ashore before too long, for she did no more fishing even though, on a dive, a large eel, her favourite food, swerved out of her way with a flick of its silvery tail. Besides, young Coire was quite a load to carry – she put that right, immediately, rolling right over and unceremoniously dumping her daughter. The little bitch, caught by surprise, swallowed water, shook her head vigorously to get rid of it, then once again fell in behind her mother.

There was one more strange happening in this voyage of discovery. In the middle of one of their mother's long, gliding dives, the cubs suddenly became aware of an enormous 'shape' looming ahead. A dark monster, with a huge body, seemed to be powering straight towards them at an alarming speed. This must be a very large fish, indeed, and it certainly meant them no good. Terrified, they caught up with their parent and drew in as close as they could to her protecting presence. But, strange! The otter bitch, though keeping a wary eye on the creature, did not seem greatly concerned. She just kept steadily swimming along and did not alter course. So, knowing no other way of staying safe, her family did the same. At the last possible moment, when a terrible collision seemed inevitable, the 'thing' veered away, regarding the little group with cool, incurious eyes, then quickly sped off into the gloom of dark and deeper waters. The otter cubs had just encountered their first seal in the water, and they would meet many more.

As the little party surfaced again, the cubs became aware of familiar scents. Shore scents! For a little while longer, the otter bitch kept swimming straight for those inviting odours which all the time grew stronger. Then she began the usual routine for going ashore. *Follow me,* she whickered softly, then dived into a welcoming world the youngsters recognised at once, the swaying, waving fronds of a seaweed forest in shallow water. A brisk paddling grounded their feet on a rocky shore and they hauled out, one after the other, at the very spot the mother had intended all the time.

The cubs quickly realised this was not Otter Cub Bay. It looked and smelled different. But Kelpie followed the usual routine. She led her family straight over the weed to a large rock some way up the shore where they spent a little while sniffing for spraint 'messages' which might have been left by other otters. Finding none, each left one of its own. Pelts all wet and sticky with salt, had now to be attended to. A great grooming took place, a wonderful rolling in the weed to squeeze out surplus water, a busy biting, nibbling and scratching until thick fur settled back into place all dry and shining. At last, after the long journey, they felt comfortable. The otter mother, knowing her offspring must be tired and hungry after all their hard work, told them to stay where they were, then trotted straight back to the water's edge. With no backward glance to check that they did not follow her, she breasted once more into the sparkling water, to hunt for a meal. The cubs pottered about for a few moments, sniffing over the rock, even starting a desultory romp, but happening upon an inviting hollow lined with seaweed, discovered that they were weary. Curling together, they promptly fell asleep.

Kelpie wasted no time in the shallows but made for deeper water where, further from the shore, the seaweed forest became dense and tall and the seabed was covered in huge rocks – good lurking places for more worthwhile prey. She did not have to search for long. A lazy flick of a tail behind a curtain of seaweed gave away the presence of a large lumpsucker. There was no hesitation. Silent and deadly, the otter darted in, seized the unaware fish and then, rising to the surface with the struggling creature in her jaws, began making for the shore. As she swam, she could hear the urgent calling from her family: *we are hungry*, and as they rushed to greet her, tripping over the slimy weed and slippery rock, even falling over each other in their anxiety to get to her first, she dropped the prey in the weed. Soon, they were squabbling over a fine fat meal.

The otter bitch returned to the sea to do some hunting for herself. In due course, when she too had fed, all three otters, companionably together, began to clean-up their cheeks, whiskers and throats on the top of a big rock. Completely restored after their long swim, Coll and Coire began a strenuous wrestling match, rolling over and over in the tangle, splashing in and out of the shallows close to where they had come ashore, and whickering at the tops of their voices with excitement. But Kelpie slid down from the rock she had been resting on and, with a quiet little chirrup of command, ambled off across the shore towards tall rocks, trees, and other familiar green 'things'. Surprised, but obedient and sensing new surroundings and a strange environment, the cubs fell in behind.

The bitch led them over a rocky terrain, just like that in the bay at home. They scampered over small rocks and oily strands of the tangle weed, waded in and out of little pools where the sea, on a rising tide, was lapping in refreshing water. Tiny fish scooted for shelter as the otter family passed and Coll was all for trying to catch one. His mother hurried him on. Then they were padding over a small beach of pebbles and this brought them to a yellow strand. The cubs had never experienced sand like this before. They found it strangely soft underfoot, not easy to walk over – four large footprints, the web clearly showing, and eight much smaller ones, patterned a way across and then were left behind till the tide would obliterate all sign of otter presence. Bigger, taller rocks decorated in orange and yellow lichens were next – here they leapt and scrambled over pitted surfaces, where cracks and tiny ledges gave purchase to urgently scrabbling claws. Just as the cubs were beginning to tire – it had been a long day, after all – the family arrived at the top of an impressive outcrop, just like the one in Otter Cub Bay.

A small grass clearing in the centre of rough heather was scattered all over with the remains of many an otter meal. It smelled nicely of their own species and fish. Kelpie carefully checked a number of spraints and found the scent good. No strange otters. To the cubs, it seemed like a good place and they would have lingered for a while. But their mother hurried them on, trotting straight over to an opening in the middle of thick, curling bracken fronds. Nose low to the ground, sniffing here, sniffing there, she led them straight along a well worn track. The cubs followed reluctantly. Surely, this was an otter place and they could stay?

On and on they continued through the bracken, the trail taking them over and around the moss-covered boulders which were strewn all over the hillside, through patches of rough, coat-scouring heather and bracken forest thick with summer's growth. Very soon, Kelpie came to a halt in another clearing, but this one was quite different.

Instead of heather and bracken, it was a smooth place of grass and moss and was surrounded by tall trees, old trees with lichens growing all over their stems – a damp place. It, too, was surely an otter location, for a pile of spraint was heaped on a patch of blackened soil by one of the trees. Behind the clearing were the fissured sides of a cliff where water tumbled down from rocky heights and ferns grew on small ledges. A jumble of enormous boulders that had fallen away from its sides was piled at the bottom.

The tall trees, their canopies swaying in a tiny breeze, made it a secret and sombre place, but the sound of the restless sea was not too far below and would prove comforting to fearful cubs. Coll and Coire looked to their mother for reassurance, wondering what she would do next. The otter bitch did not hesitate. She ran towards the craggy boulders, leaping from one to another, the cubs struggling along behind, until she came to a secret hole between two of them, an otter holt. A large, flat rock overhung it and would shelter its entrance from the worst of downpours. A small pool was there and, of course, it was reassuring to the youngsters for they were reminded of that other one that they knew so well. There was no time for play, now, however. The otter bitch dived straight into the yawning hole and the cubs followed after. They found themselves in a dimly lit cavern lined with rough rock walls, the floor covered in dead grass and bracken. Already, their mother was curling round and round to settle herself comfortably in a hollow, and Coll and Coire, exhausted after their long, exciting day, snuggled in close beside her warm body. It was just like their home in Otter Cub Bay.

Family Affairs

Entirely recovered from their long swim, Coll and Coire were on the shore early the next morning, hungry as ever and busily turning the weed to look for titbits. They had followed the scent of the day before, retracing the trail through the heather and bracken, then down over the giant rocks of the outcrop. This was just like home. The tide, in this new place, was ebbing, as it always did, the sea becoming more distant and the world of rocks and pools around them ever more extensive. A steady drizzle was falling from a leaden sky and that, too, was normal. They knew this was not Otter Cub Bay but, in a little while, when they had become used to the new surroundings, especially its scents, they would think of it as the place where they had a safe holt in the wood quite close to Oakwood Bay.

Now, on this vast new shore, they were checking each little pool and tangle-draped rock for anything that could be caught and eaten. When the sound of trickling water caught their ears, they quickly discovered a burn on its way to the sea and wandered a little way up its course. The scent was good so they continued along it and arrived, quite soon, at a kind of place they had never met with before. Instead of a rock-strewn shore, there was now a large spread of small pebbles lying on either side of the burn and stretching, it seemed, for ever towards the trees and green vegetation which fringed the bay. They could not know it but these pebbles had been thrown up by the storms of long ago but, now, were not threatened even by a high tide.

This was something different to explore, and inviting, too. Scenting busily, this way, that way, they began to traverse it and soon found something new to marvel at. Amongst the stones of this fascinating expanse, they stumbled upon small hollows and scrapes with two or three strange objects lying snugly contained within. The 'things' had an enticing smell and to the youngsters, more conscious than ever of empty stomachs, the message was clear. These could be eaten. As yet, knowing nothing of the eggs of gulls and other seabirds, but recognising an aroma that meant food, they quickly grabbed one each, found it good, and were about to seize another. There was no second helping, however. The first, a delicious tasty morsel, was hardly swallowed before pandemonium broke out. A screeching, screaming commotion of gulls came swooping and swirling about their heads and engulfed them in furiously flapping wings. Raucous voices squawked hate as the angry birds dived, and dived again, wheeling to right and left as they almost touched down, then soared away to gain height for the next assault. Coll and Coire, bewildered rather than frightened, had no idea what all the fuss was about, but knew well enough that it was time to hastily withdraw.

At this moment Kelpie, no doubt alerted by all the noise and knowing well what was going on, came galloping over the shore, as fast as an otter could. *Come on*, she called, and ran quickly down towards the sea. She waded into water unruffled by any breeze and when her family came dashing to join her, made a shallow dive into the seaweed world below. One-two and one-two again, her cubs followed her action then, all three, one after the other, popped up again much further out, where the bay met the wide-open waters of the loch. The cubs, now entirely used to this procedure in their home bay, would have been happy to start foraging for a meal right away, but the mother, looking to hunt for larger prey, continued onwards, porpoising fast through the water, each dive becoming longer than the last. Was this a long swim like the one of the day before? The cubs, faithfully trying to keep up, began to be frightened, started swimming more slowly until, at last, losing touch, gave up and began paddling aimlessly about in the still waters, not sure what they must do. A woeful 'peeping' filled the air and the sound must have easily reached the fast-vanishing parent. To no avail. She did not turn back. When finally she had been swallowed up in the grey mist of distance, where the sea became sky or the sky became sea, they couldn't tell which, they turned around and started paddling for the shore as fast as they could.

Shaking out their coats on dry land, the cubs felt safe but hungry as ever. They began pottering about, investigating the tangle strands which hung over the small rocks, turning over any likely stones in the little pools which might harbour a fish lurking beneath, but with little success. They snapped up a few small shore crabs, but these did little to fill empty stomachs. Then, all of a sudden, the lessons of previous days came to the rescue. They remembered that bigger prey could be hunted in the less shallow waters further out in the loch. There was still no sign of their mother. Hunger drove away fear. Quite soon, they were back in the water chasing the small eels, butterfish and blennies which darted this way and that in the seaweed forest some way from the shore and looked tantalisingly easy to catch – but they always seemed to be just out of reach!

Coire was the first to be lucky. A quite large butterfish was slow to see danger coming. She seized it quite expertly, but rising to the surface with the struggling creature, knew she would have to take it ashore to eat. Coll, always with an eye to the main chance, spotted her immediately. As she battled for the nearest safe landing, he tried everything he knew to make her drop her prize. All sense of direction was lost in the ensuing scuffle but the little bitch held on grimly. At last, the fish still secure, both cubs, in a flurry of foaming water, came rolling on to the weed and, at once, were engaged in a right royal battle. The little bitch, growling fiercely, hung on to her fish and would not, could not let go. The young dog, determined, grabbed the tail in his teeth, shook his head vigorously from side to side and up and down, pulled with all his strength and tried every trick he knew to make her drop it. It was a great tug of war. In the end, however, tired of getting nowhere, Coll gave up. He broke away, trotted nonchalantly back to the loch, as if the matter was of no consequence, and in a few minutes was busily foraging again. His sister enjoyed the best meal she had so far managed to land.

From out in the loch came a call: *come to me,* and it was a peremptory command which both cubs obeyed instantly. Coire ran for the water, charged in, dived quite expertly, and in only a few moments had joined her brother. Then both were swimming fast to find their mother. By now, the sun was burning the cloud away and patches of sparkling water, all ruffled in a gentle breeze, encouraged them onwards. They all met up and for a little while the air was filled with the sound of exuberant greetings and the water was churned into a cauldron of boiling, bubbling water. Not for long. Kelpie had another purpose in mind. Suddenly, she broke away and began swimming eastwards, steadily towards the sun now rising over the distant ridges. She called to her family and they, more confident now and sensing a new adventure, swam happily along behind, ready for whatever was in store.

The otter bitch was about to introduce her family to more of the place they would know as the family range, the area in which they would hunt and play, and meet the other members of the family unit. So, in a leisurely sort of way, in no hurry at all, she began to lead them along the rocky coast, mostly swimming on the surface, sometimes diving into the forest below, and never too far from land. From time to time, the cubs were allowed to rest, the whole party floating lazily in the water, Kelpie knowing that, unconsciously, they would be taking in the scents and sounds of the area and learning the subtle differences between each small bay. A pair of predatory gulls hovered overhead, following their every move and hoping, perhaps, that prey would be taken ashore. The otters were aware but seeing no threat, took no notice.

The youngsters quite quickly realised that the jutting outcrops, whose sheltering arms encompassed each bay, seemed to merit the particular attention of their parent. Whenever they approached one she changed course and swam to the shore at its base. Sometimes it was a steep and rocky climb to the top, by leaping precariously from one narrow foothold to another; sometimes there was an easier route, over the shore and up through the bracken or heather on the landward side, and always following a reassuringly otter-scented track. And these were obviously important otter places much used by others of their kind. The spraint messages were there. Comfortable 'coories' had been the resting places of other otters. Broken stalks, crushed grass, dead leaves scraped aside, all indicated energetic games of 'tig'. Coll and Coire rolled joyously in the bracken for a few moments, before following their mother down the other side and into the next bay.

Sometimes she led them ashore where no great outcrop loomed

above their heads. There, she briefly scented the weed, pottering from rock to rock, and often leaving a spraint of her own before returning to the water. It was necessary that her cubs should know every bit of their domain, which other of their species was around, which should be tolerated and which should not, and that they must leave their own spraint messages to tell the rest of the otter world that they were there. Thus, they made their way along the coast, Coll and Coire gradually learning the scents and sounds of their mother's range and becoming more and more confident with their swimming and diving skills, even their ability to catch the fish they must eat in order to survive. They certainly never worried about where they were going, or why. Instinct kept them close to Kelpie and she, the most protective of parents, made sure she was never far away.

In due course, they came to a bay where the trees of a birch wood grew right down to the shore and ancient oaks climbed the hillside – they would soon discover another holt among the trees there and use it now and again. Several large burns came tumbling down the hillside and in the wood, on more level ground, meandered around small rocks, forming large, deep pools on their way to meet the sea. Kelpie led her family to one of these and surprised them by dashing in. It seemed she had an important purpose in mind, but surely they had done enough swimming for the moment? For a few minutes, the whole family rolled and romped in the water. It felt just like being in the small pool by their home in Otter Cub Bay!

Out on the bank once more, the mother again demonstrated the importance of a good grooming, shaking herself thoroughly and giving her coat a meticulous going-over. The cubs followed suit and thus, perhaps, learned that their coats needed to be rid of salt water now and again and kept in good condition by a freshwater wash. From a favourite perch on a boulder high on the hillside a golden eagle, surveying his kingdom, observed their antics but found them of no interest. Small otter cubs could be caught and eaten when no parent was there to defend them, but, anyway, he was not hungry.

At the far end of this bay, which they would soon think of as Roedeer Bay because they kept meeting one there, the otter flotilla glided in below the most impressive outcrop they had so far encountered. It towered above their heads and was composed of

59

enormous boulders climbing to heather and bracken higher up. A small rowan, which had survived the bitter winds of many winters, crowned its summit. Kelpie led her family up the easy way from the shore and soon arrived at a smooth clearing of short grass near the top. This turned out to be an important otter place for the youngsters to learn about. All the signs were there: scent, reassuringly full of otter and fish, the ground flattened and blackened with the run-off from salt-laden coats, and the usual discarded remains of various shellfish prey. There were spraints, too, recent ones that still smelled strongly of their kind and they added their own. The cubs ran all over the place, sniffing the scent and glad to exercise their legs on dry land for a change.

In a little while, as if to return to the water of yet another bay, the otter bitch led her cubs towards the far side of the outcrop. They trotted along behind her quite happily, but when she came to a sudden halt right on the edge of a truly frightening place, they drew back aghast. Coll and Coire looked down to giant rocks, piled one upon the other, huge stepping stones leading, it seemed, to the water below. And, what water! It was a raging torrent sweeping relentlessly by, countless seething, simmering little whirlpools all tearing on the tide, rushing by with a thundering and roaring that deafened small ears. This was no place for otters! Fearfully, they retreated further from the edge of the alarming place. But then, another surprise. On the other side of this daunting water, there seemed to be another shore, similar to the one they were used to, and tantalisingly close. The youngsters, however, had never before seen water so rough and not even that inviting prospect would persuade them to enter it.

Here, in fact, was the Narrows, the narrowest part of the loch where sometimes, depending on tide and weather, the water was a turmoil of racing eddies, but could also be so calm and shallow that an otter could almost walk to the other side. In time to come, the cubs would remember it as a conveniently easy place to cross over the loch. For now, however, Kelpie had just been checking. Though her progeny would shortly be experienced enough, and strong enough, to cope with almost any sea, this was too dangerous and no place for small cubs just now. Leading them back to a good 'coorie' place on the outcrop, a hollow in a clump of bracken that she had often used before, they all curled together for a sleep. And so, their heads resting comfortably over their mother's body and feeling safe, Coll and Coire slept soundly for a while.

For the adult it was a different matter. Though she remained quite still, not disturbing her cubs, she seemed restless, sleeping only lightly, her head coming up from time to time to look around, to listen and to scent. It was as though she was expecting something special to happen. The long moments passed, the sound of distant hurrying waters was lullaby to two small cubs asleep, and the sun beat down on three recumbent forms. But then, the anticipated moment came. Suddenly, as if in a single rippling movement of her body, the otter bitch raised her head to listen, cast off her sleeping infants, and sprang to her feet. All rapt attention, she waited. A call came ringing from over the Narrows: *I am here. Let's meet.* Tangle! A sister bitch she knew well, and the other bitch in Kyle's territory.

Kelpie replied: *I am coming,* then called to the cubs to follow. Rudely awakened, but sensing a new adventure, they obeyed. The bitch led them to the top of a much easier route to the sea, where a small gully would take them to rock steps not so steep. Down below, now on the slack of the ebbing tide, the water was placid and would present no threat to her youngsters. She bounded on ahead, surefooted and with never a glance back to see if they were close behind. At the bottom, on a seaweed bed awaiting the stirring of the rising tide, she once more lifted her nose into the air, urgently checking, checking. There it was, good and strong, the scent she was looking for! Whickering her reply: *I am coming,* she plunged straight into the serene waters and set off for the far side of the Narrows. Her family, bewildered but faithful, followed after. What was all this about?

On a similar outcrop on the other side, an almost identical drama was unfolding. Tangle and her two cubs, Tarn and Torrie, were there, the young ones squabbling over a fish and the mother more concerned with what was happening across the Narrows. The urgent call came from Kelpie and, instantly, the mother bitch was running down over the rocks to the water. Fish forgotten, her family ran into the water, too. At almost the same moment, both groups shallow-dived towards a meeting in the centre of the Narrows and, rising

61

close to each other, began an ecstatic and extremely noisy greetings occasion. They all joined in and it quickly developed into a boisterous frolic. Who was chasing who seemed irrelevant. All were energetically boxing, biting, kicking, or wrestling with whoever was handy, irrespective of age, relationship or seniority. It was a game to be played as hard as otters could.

But, as so often happened in this otter world, all of a sudden and for no particular reason, they had all of them had enough. Tangle broke away and began swimming back to where she had come from and, as if an order had been given, her cubs were right behind. Kelpie with her family followed for she knew this place well. It was called Otter Point and it was a good place for otters. The climb from the sea was an easy one and Coll and Coire found no difficulty in keeping up. A short pebble ramp between two large boulders climbed up to a soft boggy area with yellow iris in its centre, and this merged into a typical otter playground of grass with small boulders dotted all over it. They hesitated for a moment, standing close to their mother and looking all around. Right behind them was a small scattering of birch trees growing on a small knoll and beyond that, dimly seen, a huge expanse of green forest climbing the steep hillside to craggy heights above. In due course, the youngsters would learn of two holts in the wood, safe places for young otters to shelter in, and of the way in there, through an old drain in the next bay. Otter Point was, indeed, a perfect haven for otters.

For now, the cubs hesitated a moment, standing close to their mother and looking all around. They were not sure what to make of another otter family, though their mother seemed happy enough and, after all, they had just been having a great game in the Narrows. They were soon reassured, however, and confidence returned. Coats were quickly shaken out, then a serious frolic began again. All the otters took part in another uproarious contest, tearing in and out of the tall stems, romping over the short grass, dodging around the small rocks, sometimes skidding away down into the slippery seaweed close to the sea, playing catch-me-if-you-can as hard as they could. It did not last too long, however. The exciting encounter in the Narrows had been exhausting for the young cubs and, in a short time, energy ran out. As if a switch had been tripped, all activity ceased. For a moment, Coll and Coire, Torrie and Tarn, remained still, as if undecided what to do next, then each wandered off to join its parent, to lick and be licked, to nuzzle, to settle beside her and to fall sound asleep.

A little while later, Tangle rose to her feet and, with a quiet command to her family, returned to the water on the far side of Otter Point, the east side. Here was a wide bay, apparently stretching for ever, far beyond the limit to which an otter could see. She was well-acquainted with it, however, for it led to the holt where her cubs had been born. She thought of it as Duck Bay, for rafts of mallard and others were often feeding there. Now with her family coming after, she began swimming across it, close to the shore, neither stopping to forage nor going ashore to explore the weed. Very purposefully, she was on her way to somewhere else and for the moment, the exciting happenings of the huge outcrop behind them, and even hunger, were of no consequence.

Meantime, Kelpie, half-asleep but noting her sister's departure, woke to an empty belly. She quietly withdrew from her sleeping cubs and with no fuss or command to them, trotted to the other side of the outcrop, the west side, and in a gentle ripple of the water, breasted in to make for home waters. A scent, coming with the tide, told her there were fish there. Coll, more alert than his sister, rose at once and ran after her, but Coire, tired out after their recent adventures, remained sound asleep in a seaweed hollow, oblivious to what was going on.

Tangle and her family continued on their way, steadily working along the shores of the bay, shallow-diving, swimming in a leisurely sort of way, but never stopping to forage. They met a mallard duck with nine ducklings bobbing in line behind. Unaware of approaching danger, she sailed serenely onwards, right across their path and only a small distance ahead. Opportunist Tarn, the young male, saw them at once, and noted the prospect of a meal. He swerved away, swam towards them and was about to dive and grab from below, when the mallard mother spotted him. Angrily, she rose in the water and with a flurry of flapping wings, scurrying feet, and outraged quacks, ran straight for the impudent creature. That was all it took. The youngster, disconcerted rather than frightened, instantly changed course and returned to his mother and the mallard flotilla resolutely continued on its way to a safer side of the loch.

Tangle's cubs, though a little older than Kelpie's, still had new adventures to experience as part of life on the loch. Only a few moments later, a huge seal came cruising up the loch, looking for rival males in competition for his harem. Just as he was passing the otter family, he heaved himself high in the air with a resounding snort, then slammed down on the water with a wallop that sent a tidal wave rolling for the shore. Both cubs squeaked in alarm and swam, as fast as they could, to be close to their mother. She was taking no notice of this peculiar event, however, so they were reassured. Above the otters, a gull, floating on silver wings, kept pace with their progress in case they went ashore with prey – titbits might be won. Two oystercatchers, with clamorous trilling, announced their fleeting arrival and departure for hunting places at the top of the loch and a pair of curlew called mournfully to each other on the nearby rocks. By now, this was all routine to the young otters and though they were aware, they took no particular notice.

In Otter Cub Bay Kelpie knew exactly where she was but Coll, feeling strange and somewhat apprehensive after all the new experiences of the morning, took a few minutes to realise he was in his home bay again. He found this both amazing and comforting, and when his parent swam off into deeper waters to forage, was happy to explore the well-known shore for eel pout and crabs, or anything else that might be there. They did little to satisfy a ravenous hunger and when Kelpie came sailing back with a large flounder, he greeted her with excited chittering: *hurry up, I'm starving*. With difficulty, she dragged the struggling thing over the shore, dropped it on the weed and then, for an interval, mother and son shared a large meal together most amicably. Neither of them seemed to notice that Coire was not there.

Meantime, on Otter Point, Coire waking from deep sleep, found no other otters on the rock beside her, and panicked. Where was her mother? Where was Coll? For a while she lifted her voice to the heavens, 'peeping' anxiously, but nothing happened. Kelpie did not come. Coll was nowhere to be seen. No comforting presence ran over the rock towards her and no reply came to her wistful calling.

The little bitch, at last desolate and hungry, wandered over the outcrop and down into the bay on the other side, Duck Bay. It was instinct to scent the shore and she soon winded her own species, not the familiar smell of her mother and sibling but, nevertheless, scent of otters. That was encouraging, so she entered the water, noted the scent again, and began swimming as fast as she could to try and catch up.

By now Tangle and her family had reached the end of the bay, at Birchwood Point, and with no hanging around to forage or play, left the water and climbed the rocks into a clearing. Here they all dried off their coats and the youngsters, tired and knowing the place well, ran straight off to their holt. In seconds, they were asleep. The bitch settled down in a 'coorie' spot close-by, and after a few desultory licks to her coat also closed her eyes. But not for long. Suddenly wide awake again, head raised, ears pricked, she was picking up the sound of a faint 'peeping' call. A cub! It came wafting through the birches and seemed to be from the loch. Now, she was scenting busily as well, and yes, this was otter cub scent. The sound came again, pathetic and insistent: *I am lost. I am hungry.* The otter bitch knew that her own cubs were safe in their holt, but her motherly instinct was strong, so she must go and investigate. Without disturbing her family, she ran back to the shore.

Tangle quickly discovered a young otter perched on one of the rocks close to the loch and calling disconsolately for its mother. She even recognised one of the cubs which had been with Kelpie. That cub was hungry! She ran into the water, dived, and in only moments came swimming ashore with a small lumpsucker. This she laid on the rock beside the distressed creature then, complacently, sat by to watch it eat. Coire was so hungry it mattered nothing that this was not her own parent and in seconds she was tearing the prey apart and greedily swallowing. But when the meal was finished, the hunger pangs gone, the little cub, once more, realised her mother was absent. She squeaked in alarm and would have run for the water. Tangle again came to the rescue. A familiar, soft command: *follow me*, restored confidence in the exhausted creature and, in a moment, she was meekly accompanying her adoptive parent over the rocks. When they arrived at the holt where Tarn and Torrie were still sleeping, she was so tired it mattered not that mother and brother were missing. She curled up beside her new friends and was instantly asleep.

Back in Otter Cub Bay, Kelpie and Coll had finished off their flounder and were companionably cleaning up each other's coats and nuzzling each other in friendly fashion. They were so contented, it was quite a long time before the bitch awoke to the fact that she only had one cub! At once dismayed, she called a sharp command to Coll, then ran as fast as she could down the shore and into the water. Remembering well the recent meeting with Tangle, she began swimming as fast as she could for Otter Point. Coll, not worried about a missing sibling but having no idea what the hurry was all about, raced to keep up. Arriving at Otter Point, they ran all over the big outcrop, checking each of its otter paths, in and out of the trees, over the grass clearing with its boggy, iris patch, and down among the rocks nearer the sea, sniffing everywhere for fresh scent. There was no sign of Coire.

Finally, they scrambled down to the shore of Duck Bay. And there it was, at last, strong scent of Coire and the other family as well. Both ran into the water and began making their way across the huge bay. The scent was good in its calm waters, but the way was slow because, all the time, it led them in and out of the shallows, even on to the shore, wherever Coire had searched in vain. Anxious now to be reunited with her cub, the mother hurried as fast as was possible and did not stop to forage. They passed a small family of ducks feeding in the seaweed shallows and Coll, like his young cousin before him, thought it a good moment to grab a meal. He was sharply ordered away.

On and on they went, the long bay gradually being traversed without incident and, at last, the scent took them to the rock-strewn shore near Tangle's holt. Kelpie knew this place well and, on occasion, had sheltered there herself. Now, instead of calling to Coire whose scent she had quickly identified, she ran up over the rocks, through the birch wood and on to the clearing beside the holt. There they found Tangle, alert and obviously expecting them. Shortly, sensing that something interesting was happening, all the cubs came tumbling out to give the new arrivals a welcome. Coire greeted her mother and brother in a matter-of-fact sort of way, as if she had never had a problem – perhaps she had just needed to feel secure in the presence of an adult. Very soon, both families made themselves comfortable in a nearby bracken bed and fell sound asleep.

A Dog's Life

An eeried stillness held the loch in limbo. Mist hung low over the world of the otters, imprisoning hillsides, woods and forest, and rocky shores in impenetrable curtains of clinging moisture. Nature wept. Teardrops gathered, multiplied, overflowed, and fell relentlessly to the sodden earth beneath. No vision could penetrate that smothering mantle, except for the sharpest of eyes. No distant sound could be heard, except by the most sensitive of ears. No scent could be picked up, for it was held in suspension, waiting for a breeze. Silence enfolded the tranquil waters of the loch, prohibiting all knowledge of the world beyond. But then … what was this? A tiny 'plop' in that untroubled seascape. A rippled circle spreading over its mirrored surface. From what undetected source? A long, tapering tail on the end of a disappearing body was, in fact, an otter diving. Near the top of the loch, where Kyle had a favourite holt, the dominant dog of the range headed into the tangle forest below to forage for a meal.

Kelpie, resting with her family in the holt at Otter Point, was hearing a different sort of sound – a thin, wistful crying as of a small creature in distress. She recognised it at once. On the skerrie rocks of a nearby island, pregnant seal mothers had recently been giving birth to their pups and, soon, that single cry would become a mournful ululation of many voices, breaking through the all-enveloping mist and echoing around the loch. There were many pups on the rocks and Coll and Coire must be reminded that they should always give protective seal mothers a wide berth. In the holt at Oakwood Bay, Tangle also was hearing that rising crescendo of woe and knew well what it meant. She, too, must keep her youngsters away from the seal skerries.

Kyle caught a lumpsucker. It was a large one so he took it ashore to the nearest rock point. He was in the middle of his delicious meal when, all of a sudden, he heard something that caused him to bring his head up sharply to listen. A faint sound was wafting through the mist and echoing over the water. With a paw to hold his fish secure, he listened hard and 'pointed' every which way in order to pick up scent. It came again, drifting on the hint of a breeze through the dense curtains of mist, the lugubrious chorus that his bitches were hearing. At once, he relaxed. That mournful wailing would become the clamorous outcry of many anxious infants, all trying to make contact with their mothers. It was the time of the seal pups and of no great concern to him. But he would not swim too close to those skerries.

The sorrowful sound, however, had served a purpose. It reminded the dog of his territorial duties. Both Kelpie and Tangle had young families and it was time to check the loch for intruders. Abandoning his fish, he climbed a small rock nearby to deposit a spraint to say: *this is my place.* Then he trotted back into the water and, after a short, shallow dive, surfaced in the middle of the nearest bay. Floating on his back, he tested the tide and felt it slowly taking him the way he must go. So he rolled right way up and allowed it to carry him towards the next outcrop down the loch and, in a matter of moments, was treading water in the shallows beneath it. Standing tall on his hindlegs, he rose to look around and to test for alien scent, but there was nothing that bothered him. Better check on the top. Leaping from one broad ledge to another, an oft-used otter route on this fortress rock, he quickly reached the summit. He pottered all over the familiar top, with its blackened vegetation where otters often brought their prey and sometimes groomed their coats, sniffing carefully for scent or spraint – of friend or foe. He found nothing fresh and after depositing his own message: *I have been here*, he bounded down the other side into the next bay.

Here was a large rock, flat-topped and draped on each of its sides in luxuriant strands of the tangle. Too tall to be covered by the sea, except at spring tides, it was a favourite place for otters to mark.

Better investigate. But no message was there, so he deposited his own, then jumped down again. A huge pile of seaweed held a promising scent of a titbit, but scraping busily away he found nothing. He paddled through a shallow pool – a shore crab or two might be hiding in the tangle, but they were not. So he sauntered back into the sea and, being in no particular hurry but always happy to catch opportune prey, began foraging in the shallows. His prize was a blenny, expertly seized, and a small eel caught unawares. Both could be demolished without going ashore. Satisfied for the moment, he lay floating on his back, forelegs clasped to his breast, hind legs pointing to the skies, allowing the tide to bear him along. No scent to worry about, his stomach comfortable, there was all the time in the world.

At last, after a leisurely progress across the loch, Kyle found himself below Birchwood Point. Here was where the loch became narrow, either side only a short swim away. Soon he would be sailing through those Narrows, visiting rock points and seaweed-covered shores, breaking his journey to investigate any suspicious scent which would indicate an intruder. For the present, he was bent on a social call for here was Tangle's holt, the one in which she had reared her cubs. He came gliding ashore through the tangle, gave himself a brisk shaking, then moseyed all over the surrounding rocks to sniff for scent. There was plenty of it and, surely, that of his bitch and her family.

He climbed higher on the bank, springing easily from one rock to another on the customary route from the shore to the grassy clearing in the wood. Here, a large hole beneath a sheltering boulder, was her holt. A small distance away, Kyle whickered a soft greeting. Then another, more insistent. But there was no reply. Without further delay, he ran down to the loch again. Tangle was not at home.

The tide was gathering speed, now, and whirlpool water began to scurry him through the Narrows. Kyle glided merrily along, mostly on his back, taking life easily and only rolling over to correct direction when he needed to go ashore. The mist had vanished and a bright sun shone on sparkling water hurrying to join the big open sea in the west. He found no alien scent to concern him, just the lingering scent of both his families who had seemingly been around quite recently. Though he could hear the seal pups on the skerries, lifting soulful cries to the heavens, their song was muted in the rushing waters and worried him not at all. All was well with his world.

In Otter Cub Bay, Kelpie was foraging for a meal and had already sensed that the dog otter was on his way. There had been no hint on the air of his coming, for the breeze would be wafting it up the loch, but on the ebbing tide had come a scent that she instantly identified. Now she swam fast for a vantage rock on Otter Point from where she could watch the turbulent waters. She would greet her mate when he came.

Way down the loch, in Oakwood Bay, Tangle as yet had no knowledge of the dog's progress through the Narrows. She was snoozing in a coorie place in the bracken while her cubs were down in the shallows, nearby, hunting for crabs and the like. In a little while she would lead them along the shores of the loch towards Roedeer Bay, foraging as they travelled but with bigger prey in mind in the waters between it and the Seal Island skerries opposite. She was well aware of the seal nursery so close – even now she could hear the melancholy chorus – and would see to it that they did not venture too near.

Nearing the end of the Narrows on his whirling, swirling journey, Kyle already knew that he would go ashore on Otter Point, for he had scented Kelpie and her family there. Rock Point opposite must be visited, as well, for here the loch was at its most narrow and both outcrops were much used hauling out places for otters. It, too, must be inspected for scent of an interloper.

On Otter Point, all of a sudden, Kelpie was running as fast as an otter could over the clearing in the birches, galloping over the wide, pebble ramp which separated forest from the Point and clumsily scrambling from one rock to another in her hurry to return to the loch. Coll and Coire, waking up in the holt and sensing something exciting about to happen, came scurrying after her. The bitch whickered an imperious message: *I am here,* and Kyle, only a short distance away, replied: *I am coming.*

On the other side of the loch, in Roedeer Bay, Tangle heard the exciting exchange and added her voice to the urgent messages: *I am here, I am coming.* She called to Tarn and Torrie, who were squabbling over a fish, and then her own small flotilla was making for the Narrows as quickly as they could dive and swim through the surging waters.

Into the seaweed forest of the narrowest part of the Narrows, Kyle, Kelpie and Tangle, at almost the same moment, dived deep on a course to meet, and one, two, three, four, the cubs followed suit. Seven otters, the three adults each with the same objective in mind and their cubs with no idea at all of what was happening, but taking on the infectious action of their mothers, rose as one to welcome each other. Then whickering delight at the tops of their voices, they turned the Narrows into a witch's cauldron of foaming water. The rapturous greetings became a rumbustious game played to the limits of otter ingenuity and strength. In and out of the swaying stems they streaked, effortless bending of supple sleek bodies, adults and youngsters alike, chasing and being chased, swooping after the nearest fleeing body, soaring to the surface for a gulp of air, wrestling, boxing, biting, corkscrewing over and round whichever furry creature was to hand. All the world in nature must have known about this tumultuous meeting, so great was the noise.

Gradually, the initial excitement died down and, instead, became a different kind of drama. The cubs found themselves playing the game in a more desultory fashion and their parents were no longer interested. Any attempt to engage with them received a growl and a snap from wicked teeth: *keep away*. Kyle had discovered the scent of each of his bitches exciting and stimulating. They might soon be ready to mate. He began to court each in turn, swimming close alongside, nuzzling and nudging their sleek bodies, even attempting to mount one or the other. But the time was not ripe. Neither would permit any liberties. Kyle, frustrated, was the first to break off the encounter. He turned away, diving deep into the forest below, kicked hard for the wide open loch beyond the Narrows … and disappeared. The bitches, noting his sudden absence and tired themselves, called to their cubs. Kelpie, with Coll and Coire, began the long journey to the holt in Oakwood Bay and Tangle, deciding it was time for a rest, led her family on to the rocks of Otter Point. She followed her sister's strong scent to the holt and Tarn and Torrie soon settled beside her. It had been a great get-together.

Kyle surfaced in the waters between Roedeer Bay and the seal skerries. He rocked on the wavelets for a while, revolving slowly with the current, content that the sun, blazing from the infinite blueness above, should be warming his stomach. The young seal pups were swelling the mournful chorus on the skerries but, though dimly aware of the coronach crescendo, he was not in the least concerned. They were of no interest to him. However, he did soon discover he was hungry. No sooner had the thought occurred than he rolled over in the rippling water, dived below into a sun-dappled world of golden sand and rocks all covered in the tangle, and began to hunt. Here, the fishing was often good. He might catch a big one.

As long as his breath permitted, the dog coasted slowly over a sandy bottom studded with small islands of rock, gliding in and out of shadow and golden light, depending more on the vibrations picked up by his sensitive whiskers than on his poor eyesight to locate his quarry. Each dive was a deep one and each progress leisurely and long, but no unwary fish lay motionless on the bottom nor lurked in the shelter of a rock. Just as he was about to abandon the hunt and make for more productive waters, he spotted a slight stirring in the quicksilver sand, looked again and saw a tail slowly oscillating, gently disturbing the golden grains. The flounder had no chance. The otter was down in a flash and in seconds was shooting for the surface. He broke through the ruffled water, the flapping fish safely held in his jaws … and got a rude surprise. The skerries! The seals! Fish now gripped in his paws, he looked hastily all around, almost overwhelmed by the cacophony – and received another shock. Right beside him, an attentive mother was lying beside her young pup. He was right in the middle of the seal colony and, certainly, too close for comfort or safety.

Much too close! An indignant bellow heralded action. Pup rudely cast aside, the mother began laboriously hauling herself down the rock in order to deal with the intruder. Kyle did not hang around. As the great body slid into the sea, he dropped his prey, dived deep and long, then began swimming for dear life out into the wide waters of the loch. The enormous creature came powering after him – superior in speed but with a body that responded more slowly to the otter's every move. It was an unequal contest. Jinking this way and that, twisting and turning, soaring up towards the surface, catapulting down into the depths, the agile otter taunted his adversary and avoided her cumbersome lunges. Very soon, he was way out of reach.

The angry parent gave up – her protest had just been a gesture, anyway! She turned around and slowly made her way back to her young. The dog otter resumed his foraging right in the centre of the loch. It had all happened many times before in other seasons and he had not been greatly put out. Within minutes, the episode completely forgotten, he had caught a large eel, his favourite prey, and was swimming for Roedeer Bay. At last ashore with the slippery creature, he tore great chunks from the still-squirming body and chomped on the juicy morsels. Each mouthful was hardly swallowed before he was ripping away another piece. That eel tasted excellent!

It should have been a good feeding undisturbed by any other creature – even the marauding hoodie crows had so far not discovered him. But, suddenly, a piece of eel still dripping in his jaws, the dog raised his head to listen. What was this? A thin 'peeping' sound came wafting over the shore from the far end of the bay. One of his cubs? The call came again, plaintive and distressed: *I am hungry, I am lost*. The message was clear and Kyle responded at once, for he could not help it. Picking up the remainder of his fish, he trotted back into the water and began swimming purposefully towards the pathetic sound.

It was Coire. After the great meeting at Otter Point, she had followed both mother and sibling on their journey down the loch, but in Roedeer Bay she had dived after a tempting fish. Deep down, in clear water over a sandy bottom, she had suddenly become aware of a young seal, apparently after the same prey. For a couple of seconds, both continued speeding towards a large flounder. Then either curiosity or rivalry being the spur, the seal performed a graceful arc in the water and came streaking towards her. Fish forgotten, Coire swerved out of the way, rose to the surface for a quick gulp of air, then dived for the shore as fast as she could. Safely there, she shook out her coat and started looking around for her family. No mother. No brother. Neither could be seen, scented nor heard. After long moments, when they did not turn up, she grew frightened and had begun her pathetic calling. When Kyle came sailing out of the sea to lay a lump of delectable eel in front of her, she saw only a large otter who smelled vaguely familiar and was coming to her rescue. It didn't matter at all which otter. She grabbed the fish greedily and the dog sat beside her, scratching his coat, while she polished it off.

Kelpie did, at last, come looking for her daughter. Coasting round the point from the next bay along, pausing frequently to scent and listen, she at once picked up the scent of both dog and cub. *I am coming*, she whickered and came gliding ashore through the tangle. Once again, the dominant dog otter greeted his bitch, whickering his pleasure and briefly nuzzling into her thick fur flanks. Again, there was no response, so rebuffed once again, he trundled down to the water and breasted in. The bitch led her daughter, now sleek and satisfied, to the holt in the next bay where Coll was still sleeping off his energetic romp.

Kyle continued his patrolling duties. The tide was still ebbing, the sun on its descending arc to the west, and the mist of the morning already beginning to form once again. The seal pups were quiet, perhaps asleep beside their mothers. Somewhere, a heron squawked angrily, he didn't know why. Above his head, gulls floated languidly on the air, occasionally uttering weird cries to each other and each on its way to an evening roost. It was all very peaceful and routine and very soon he would come to the end of the territory he defended. He began to swim for its last rugged outcrop.

Oakwood Bay held the last of the holts that his bitches would use. Beyond was a part of the loch where otters from other territories were sometimes encountered. There, also, the grown-up cubs – the young sub-adults of the previous breeding season, his own and others – would forage, find holts in which to rest, sometimes play or scrap, until the time came when they, too, must look for vacant territories and mates. Other male otters held dominion further down the loch, on the way to the open sea, and he would not venture there. The dog otter skirted the base of the first outcrop that sheltered the bay. An impudent seal had hauled out there and recent experience in mind, he gave it a wide berth. There was no scent of an intruding otter, however, so he paddled slowly along in the shallows, always watching, listening and scenting.

Kyle had arrived at the place he was making for. Edged with the oak of an ancient wood, he knew it well. A small burn hurried to the sea. He scrambled up its damp, moss-lined gully, brushing the ferns aside, then shook himself energetically at the top. Beneath an old tree, one of many before the boulder-strewn ground became a rocky cliff, was a much used playground of his cubs and nearby, right in the centre of the big rocks, was the dark entrance to a holt. He noted a recently deposited spraint beside it. Kelpie's! In the warm sunshine of evening and satisfied that all was well with his world, Kyle curled on a thick bed of moss, to sleep. He would continue his patrolling when the tide had turned.

Small Happenings in a Growing-Up

Strange fish

Coll and Coire came paddling into Otter Cub Bay. They were all on their own, though Kelpie was not far away on the far side of Otter Point, where she had just eaten a large fish and was grooming her coat. The young otters knew this place well, its every pool and tangle-covered rock was familiar. Above them loomed the giant buttress rock which contained their birthplace and which, even now, they occasionally visited. The trails through the bracken and heather were still there, not so well-used, but well remembered and holding the faint scent of their family. The climb from the sea, that alternative way up through a narrow, steep gully which had once seemed so hard had become routine and whenever they were there could be scrambled up quite easily. They were fine, healthy youngsters, now.

The cubs began a romp, the usual zestful exchange of chasing, nipping and wrestling in the shallows. Then, bored with that, they swam for deeper water, diving down into the tangle forest to continue the game, in and out of its swaying stems, over the shell and seaweed covered boulders on its bottom, dodging in and out of dappled sunshine and shadow. A host of small creatures scurried and scuttled out of their way.

The mood changed and suddenly they were swimming for the shore. Breaking through the gently slapping wavelets to haul out on to a favourite rock, they surprised a heron poised on a pinnacle nearby. The startled bird stepped ungainly backwards, lost its balance, and its dignity, but with urgently flapping wings regained its perch.

It haughtily regarded the clumsy intruders but they, now well-used to these creatures, were only dimly aware of its discomfiture. They began to groom their coats.

It was while they were busily attending to fur all streaky with the salt of the sea that both cubs, in the same moment, became aware of two mysterious objects far out in the bay. They had never seen anything like them before. Not too alarmed, even though the two peculiar 'things' seemed to be swimming towards them, bouncing jauntily over the water and making good speed on the rising tide, they were immediately curious. Tarn and Torrie? Certainly not. Young seal pups? No. Danger? They had no idea. Curiosity, as always, prompted action. They must find out.

Of prime importance, of course, was the need to know if these 'things' could be caught and eaten. Tumbling back into the sea they set off to find out, diving as one, kicking for deeper water, swooping up from below, and arriving quite close. But the 'creatures' took no notice, did not take fright, did not swim away, just bobbed steadily along, riding on the small wavelets and, seemingly, totally unalarmed by the arrival of the young otters. At a safe distance, the cubs paddled round and round, cautiously assessing, scenting, looking, listening and becoming more and more surprised. But, there was still no reaction from the intruders. With wary eyes watchful for the slightest threatening move, Coll and Coire waited for something to happen.

Nothing did happen. In a little while, reassured and greatly daring, Coll darted towards the nearest one and tried to grab it in his jaws. It avoided his eager strike, sliding away, dipping momentarily from sight, then popping up again on the surface out of reach. Seeing her sibling safe, Coire made for the other one, snapping vicious jaws as she came up with it, but with the same result. Frustrated, now, and spurred on by the taunting ways of these peculiar fish, both cubs joined in the fray. With thrusting limbs, flipping tails, and teeth at the ready, they sped after the tantalising creatures, soaring up from beneath the waves to surprise and grab, tearing after them on the surface. But, always, they danced out of the way, cheekily, mockingly, slipping away on the tide, always just too far away to seize ... you won't catch us.

But, in the end, the young otters came sailing ashore, triumphant.

They had not managed to capture either of the slippery creatures but each had managed to stay alongside one. Then with a nudge from their inquisitive noses, they found that they could prod, push and patiently manoeuvre the obstinate things in the direction of the shore. In due course, and almost exhausted, they were there. Each of the peculiar fish was propelled on to the tangle and then nodded, ever so carefully, into a convenient crevice between two rocks. Now, they could be grabbed and held … and eaten! Sharp teeth sank in for a mouthful … and … each mouthful was spat out with difficulty and disgust! These fish were not good to eat! The taste and texture horrible, the youngsters tried vigorously shaking their heads, hoping to get rid of the horrible, rubbery things.

Free of them at long last and instantly bored with their unrewarding prey, Coll and Coire decided to make for the old holt. They scrambled up the scree-strewn gully, sniffed over the clearing in the heather to see who had been there before them, then curled together in a hollow in the bracken. In seconds, they were sound asleep. On the shore, below, two ancient tennis balls, torn, tooth-marked, sea-stained, and forlorn, lay abandoned and forgotten. They would vanish with the next ebbing tide.

A touch of gold

In Roedeer Bay, tiny wavelets caressed the shores and with each curling surge of the tide briefly parted the tangle stems. Birch and oak leaves, sparse now on denuding branches, shivered yellow and brown in the hint of a breeze. Side by side, in the comfortable water, Coll and Coire flowed lazily along on the current, stretching their cramped limbs after a spell in a holt, not hungry, as yet, but ready to pounce should the opportunity occur.

And, it did. Floating slowly over a sandy bottom dappled in sunshine shades of gold, they suddenly spotted a tiny movement. Quite close to a solitary rock, there was a secret stirring. A small cloud of particles rose in the water then fell back into the anonymity of its surroundings. A fish! In a flash, both youngsters were streaking down. Coll expertly caught and held a large flounder and both otters, Coire right alongside, kicked for the surface. The fish still on board, the dog grabbed its head, the bitch its tail, and a small tidal wave came racing for the shore. They coasted in together, each determined not to let go, then rose out of the water through the dripping weed. With difficulty, they dragged the flailing fish on to a nearby rock and, of course, a tug-of-war immediately ensued. It was quickly over for it was a big fish and there was plenty for both. Each seized a bite and swallowed it down. Serious eating had begun.

So busy were the youngsters with this splendid meal that they failed to take note of a warning. A hoodie crow, perched on a branch close-by, observing them and weighing up the possibilities of a free meal, all at once uttered a raucous cry and took off across the loch. By now, well-accustomed to these noisy birds, the cubs heard the protest, glanced up briefly, then resumed their ravenous eating. But the crow had flown for a good reason. An awesome bird, with wings broad and long, was soaring high overhead, its head down and sharp eyes examining the shore below. It began to sink lower and lower right above the cubs and, finally, with down-stretched legs and talons spread, landed on a knife edge of rock not far away. It wobbled precariously on its perch, then settled.

The youngsters recoiled in surprise, then froze. They had never met one of these birds before. Instinct told them that movement might trigger action on the part of this impressive predator, so they crouched as low as they could to the weed and hoped their camouflage coats made them invisible. The fish was abandoned.

With unblinking eyes, the young eagle solemnly regarded the otter cubs and the prey between them. Piercing eyes assessed for several moments, but it was not really hungry, so it began to preen instead. The razor-sharp bill meticulously parted the feathering on back and breast, removing all dirt and dust, then smoothed it back into place. From time to time, it paused to look at the cubs but, mostly, it just ignored them. They were of no particular interest at the moment.

Coll and Coire resumed their meal for this big, strange bird seemed to mean them no harm. They began squabbling noisily over the last few scraps … and thereby triggered action. Diving in for the last skinny piece, the young dog gave his sister a vicious bite on her nose. Of course she squealed with pain and rage and the great bird, taken completely by surprise, nearly fell off its perch. With fast flapping wings, it just managed to recover, but, in turn, this commotion had disturbed the cubs. This was danger! They raced for the sea, stumbling over the slippery weed and threw themselves in with a resounding splash. In a series of little short dives – it was too shallow for anything else – they arrived a safe distance out in the bay. There, they paddled cautiously up and down waiting to see what the giant bird would do.

From high over a nearby ridge came a call, plaintive and piercing. A dark speck in the sky was gliding round and round on majestic wings in the sunshine of a beautiful day. The call came again, still sweet but perhaps with an imperative as well. The young eagle responded at once. Otters forgotten, it spread its wings, flapped vigorously for take-off, then, safely airborne, rose to meet its parent. Two eagles now, one gloriously golden, the other a darker brown with pale patches on wings and tail, joyously soared and swooped, rolled and tumbled, then spiralled upwards in the azure heavens, to dive again. All the time, they called one to the other, a plaintive song yet content. Higher and higher they spiralled until, at last, they vanished away to the west.

But, Coll and Coire did not return to the shore.

Predators with wings

Snow lay thick and crisp on the ground in Roedeer Bay. Fresh from a sleep in a nearby holt, Coll and Coire emerged into this strange white world. It sparkled in bright sunshine and dazzled their eyes and was bitterly cold. Very cautiously, they patted the white stuff with their paws, scraped it aside, found it intriguing and something they must immediately explore. So they pottered around on the top of the outcrop, sniffed everywhere for scent but found nothing of particular interest, and rolled in the powdery substance. It was a nice experience burrowing into its soft whiteness with their noses, only to discover familiar ground beneath. Then they set off for the shore.

But the usual way was nowhere to be found. It seemed to have vanished beneath this white mantle concealing their world, though they could scent and sense it somewhere beneath their feet. So they padded on cautiously, one carefully following in the tracks of the other, and turning the smooth, ordered whiteness into a ruffled untidiness. Noses down, checking all the time for warning scent, and sneezing now again when they sniffed too hard, they finally arrived at the top of the narrow gully which was the way to the sea. Right now, though, it had become a long, icebound furrow, with the snow frozen solid in the bitter night and the jagged rocks on either side black against the pristine backdrop.

The cubs hesitated, observing this new state of affairs with trepidation. Was it safe? Should they find another way? But Coll, always the more confident and wanting to be first, leapt boldly on to the steep ice slope … then found himself skidding away on his stomach, completely out of control, and scrabbling desperately with his claws to stop his headlong flight. He reached the bottom in a flurry of ice, pebbles and powdered snow but was lucky enough to land safely on a soft bed of seaweed. Coire, as ever more timid, noted her brother disappearing in a fluffy ball of white but appearing again, apparently unhurt, on the shore below. She would not be left behind. First, she patted the snow warily with her paw, decided it would do her no harm, then one step at a time, extended the whole of her body on to the polished surface. Whoosh! She, too, with frantic paws vainly braking, was hurtling down to land safely in the tangle.

Both youngsters, having discovered they were all in one piece, decided this was an excellent game. So they made their way back to the top of the gully, by an easier route, and played it again and again. One after the other they raced down that slide, sometimes on all fours, often rolling over and over out of control, but always landing comfortably on the seaweed mattress below. It was a great game that they might have played for a long time but, eventually, after all this energetic exercise, hunger became a gnawing demand that they could not ignore. The game was over. When he landed at the end of his last hilarious slithering, Coll discovered Coire already swimming out of the bay towards the deeper waters in the centre of the loch. He slipped into the water, too, but did not attempt to join her. Instead, he made his way round into Oakwood Bay, to forage there. As was happening more and more these days, the young cubs, growing towards adulthood and becoming more independent of each other, did not meet again for quite a while. Each had its own life to lead.

The young bitch was now a skilled hunter and it was not long before she was dragging a large eel on to the rocks – too big and lively to control in the water, she must bring it ashore to eat. In the warming sunshine the snow was slowly thawing and already, near the sea, there was a broad band of glistening seaweed uncovered. Coire dropped her prize and began giving her coat a good shaking out. Alas for Coire. An otter with a shining brown coat on a carpet of seaweed was excellent camouflage, but her magnificent fish, that hard won prey, lay pale, silvery and enormous against the tangle.

Fishing that morning had been poor for a certain hungry heron. From the topmost branches of a tree in the wood, the ravenous bird had watched the otter bringing the fish ashore and now regarded that seductive object with calculating eyes. It lifted from its perch with a great flapping of powerful wings, then began a long, gliding flight towards a meal. Coire, though deeply engaged in tearing apart and eating her prize, heard that loud rustling in the wood and the subsequent protest of a creaking branch. Startled, her head jerked up just as the great bird came flying in. It landed on a pinnacle of rock close by. She saw dark wings being settled into place along its back, spindle legs anchoring more securely on a knife edge, then greedy eyes immediately directed to her eel. This predator was far too close for comfort!

By now, the young otter was well acquainted with herons. They lined the shores of the loch at regular intervals and were usually to be seen motionless, patiently waiting for prey to come their way. Sometimes, when a small tidal wave brought an otter ashore with a fish, they backed off with a haughty high-stepping then stood, intimidating presences close by, overseeing the feast and planning to snatch a bite if they could. Though respectful of this large bird, the little bitch knew well what it had come for but had no intention of giving up any of her hard won meal. With difficulty, she gathered it back into her jaws and began to haul it further along the shore.

The ungainly heron hopped down from its perch and, step by careful step, began stalking the otter over the tangle. And with the awkward burden held fast in her jaws, the little bitch, slipping and sliding on the greasy weed, was so taken up with the business of hanging on to it that she did not at first realise a predatory presence. She paused for a rest and to shake her fish into more secure hold. The heron stopped at once, came to a halt a step or two behind. The otter continued on her way, quite unaware, determined to select a good place in which to drop her prey. Heron shadowed otter, silent and very close, padding softly over the slippery weed, right along the rough edge of the shore. The young bitch arrived at a likely spot, a hollow between two rocks where her eel would be safe. She dropped it and, immediately, dived in to tear and eat. It was only when she brought her head up, the better to swallow a large morsel, that she saw the heron. That heron meant business!

Coire was not ready to give up. She was hungry. With difficulty, she picked up the remains and dragged them a short distance over the slippery weed. But now, those remains were an awkward load, a large fish still, but torn and shredded into pieces difficult to hold together. Once again, she had to drop the impossible encumbrance. And, this was the moment. As she stretched her neck to ease its discomfort, the heron struck, a secret step from behind and a lightening stab with a wicked bill. Taken by surprise, the otter recoiled but reacted at once. Angry and quite unafraid, she flew at the would-be thief, hissing hate, growling, and ready to use her teeth.

At that very moment, four mallard drakes, all in dull winter plumage, dipping low and scolding noisily, *quark, quark, quark, quark,* flew from nowhere over the disputing pair. Startled, the heron took off with a frantic flapping of its wings and a protesting, *quaaark quaaark* of annoyance, to try for better luck in another place. The otter, as if nothing untoward had been happening, resumed her much-needed meal.

In the wood above the shore, two hoodie crows at the top of a silver birch had been watching this drama. With the heron's departure, they saw an opportunity. *Qua..ark, qua..ark, qua..ark,* they spoke, short and sharp. Then silently, stealthily, they took off from the bare, spindly branches. Now, two dark birds were flying round and round above the otter's head, assessing the situation, making up their minds, waiting for the moment. The little bitch sensed disturbance in the air above and looked up to see two enemies whose predatory ways she knew well. Greybacks! Hoodie crows with thieving in mind! She secured her fish with a paw and waited to see what would happen.

With only a whisper of their wings, the hoodies landed softly on the weed and, meaning business, began at once to sidle slowly, step by cautious step, nearer to the young otter whenever her head was down. Suddenly, one of them, with a hop, skip and a jump and a lightening stab with its bill, darted in to try for a piece. Coire, growling fiercely, drew back with a snarl, most of the fish in her mouth: *this is mine*, then stood ready to defend it to the end. With indignant squawks, both hoodies rose in protest but, persistent as ever, hopped only a few feet away. One seized a scrap lying a little apart on the weed then flew off, triumphant. The second began another stealthy approach. Head tilted to one side, beady eyes fixed on its target of succulent fish, it sideways stepped until at last it was close. The otter raised her head to chew on a mouthful and the greyback, seizing the moment and somehow avoiding bared teeth and urgent claws, succeeded in tearing away a sizeable portion. Victorious, it flew off to join its mate.

As if this experience was all in the day's work and quite normal, Coire carried on with her meal – there was still a large piece of eel

to finish off. But, yet again, when she brought up her head the better to hold and chew the fish, she discovered two more large birds standing by on the rocks. Putting on an act of being more interested in the view than her fish, two black-backed gulls, haughty and predatory, were sizing up the possibilities. But the youngster knew all about these birds. Their strategy was always to appear disinterested, as if they had no designs on her prey and were there just to clean up when she had finished. In an unguarded moment, they would pounce.

Suddenly, perhaps because all this attention had become too much for the young adult, or maybe because she had eaten her fill, Coire dropped the tattered remains of her fish, pottered nonchalantly over the weed on her way to the sea, then breasted into the tranquil waters as if she had not a care in the world. The two gulls polished off the left-overs.

A bushy tail

Winter was slow to let go its grip. The snow was deep and the frost was keen enough to freeze it into an impenetrable blanket smothering all that lay beneath. The birds and animals of the loch and surrounding hillsides were having a tough time finding enough food to stay alive. But at last the sun broke through the sullen overcast, temperatures rose a little and in favoured patches the snow began to melt away. It was enough. All hungry creatures stirred, wherever they might be, and set off to find food. A small vole struggled from its hole beneath a bush and went a-hunting for a nibble of grass. A pine marten popped its head out of its den in a tree trunk and with sharp little nose began searching for promising scent of bird or beast. A mink, black as night, and a stoat in ermine, each surveyed its world for the possibility of a meal, the one from its rocky lair beside a burn and the other from the top of an old wall bisecting the wood. Three buzzards, circling over the trees, called mournfully to each other, hungry and eager to spot an unwary creature below. Higher above them still, strangely menacing in a clear blue sky, a huge dark bird, a sea eagle, glided over the white world beneath.

There were no problems for otters, as yet, because there were plenty of fish and only at the head of the loch was it frozen over. In fact, on the tangle-bedecked shores of Roedeer Bay, now freshly washed by the tide and gleaming in the sunshine, Coll and Coire were amicably sharing a large lumpsucker. The young male had caught it and there was plenty for both. Two hoodie crows and a gull stood at a respectful distance weighing up the possibilities of a stolen meal. The otter pair noted the passing of the eagle overhead but seemed unaware of a potential competitor for their prey. They continued happily to eat.

In the winter-battered oak woods above Roedeer Bay, tired after a long night's hunting without success, a dog fox lay sleeping in a cavern on the hillside. From time to time he stirred uneasily, the hunger pangs beginning to bite. Then he was wide awake. With a big yawn, he rose at once, stretched his long limbs to the very end of his fine bushy tail, then scratched an itchy place on his side. At the entrance to his retreat, he surveyed his white world, all sparkling in dappled sunshine and shadow on the woodland floor. Then he began testing the air for promising scent. But there was nothing, no elusive aroma that told him of a good meal that he could stalk and kill. So he set forth to quarter the hillside for anything that might help to fill his stomach.

In and out of the gnarled old oaks the dog fox padded. No crack of a twig nor a stone sent skidding away would give away his presence. Nosing here, nosing there, scraping aside the snow for what might be underneath, sharp eyes checking for anything that moved, sharp ears ready to pick up the tiniest sound, he searched diligently for a meal. A sparrowhawk, also looking for prey, flew deadly and silent among the woody branches, hoping for an unwary blackbird or thrush. Reynard ignored it. Though he had, from time to time, caught a small bird on the wing, this one he would not even attempt. He picked up the scent of a vole and noting its spoor in the snow, followed both scent and footprints until he lost his quarry in a small hole on a bank of fern. He scraped away busily at the tiny opening, but to no avail because the ground was frozen still. So he continued prowling softly, softly over the woodland floor, silent, observant, intent on a meal.

A strong smell suddenly assailed his nose, pungent and unmistakable. It caused his whiskers to twitch with excitement and the muscles to tense in the whole of his long, lean body. This was, surely, CAT! A few more steps and he came to the delicate prints, clear and pristine in the snow, that gave away its passing. He paused a moment, tail flicking tentatively from side to side, remembering a recent scrap over a carcase. The cat, not too much smaller than himself, had fought furiously over the prey, spitting hate and defiance, claws bared to tear. In the end, it had slunk away, leaving him the winner but with a nasty gash on his cheek.

But these prints were small and dainty. This must be a lesser animal. He was very hungry. Here was possible prey. Using his nose to check, he hurried on, the scent becoming stronger with every moment. Then, all of a sudden, he saw it, a young cat, only a short distance away. It was crouching beside the roots of an old tree, intently watching something on the ground. The fox knew it would probably be a mouse, but he was after bigger prey, if he could catch it.

Stealthily, he crept nearer and nearer, then gathered himself for a spring …and gave the game away. The sound was tiny, but the cat heard him at once. It wasted no time, but shot up the riven stem of the ancient tree and, driven by panic, clawed its way right to the top. From a sturdy branch it glared down with fierce green eyes, hackles raised and spitting hate. Reynard, on the ground, considered a chase, for he was a good climber of trees, but knew at once that he had little chance of catching a creature more agile than he in a tree. Disappointed, he turned away.

In a little while, and still hungry, the big dog fox was fast approaching the end of the wood. Here the birches and oaks were more thinly scattered and there were small clearings of heather dressed in snow white. He sat down beside a big boulder to consider what he would do next. The shore at low water was worth hunting for titbits, something he often did when desperate for a meal, and crabs, when surprised by a scraping paw in the seaweed, were quite easily caught and good to eat. But instinct told him that was a lot of energy spent for a small reward, one which would not keep him going for long. He needed something much bigger. It was when he stood again and was about to return to the wood that his nose received a strong message. Fish! Salmon!

Reynard's nose had told him the direction. Now he crouched low, carefully checking the seaweed shore to see where the fish was lying, and if any creature would defend it. In among the tangle, cleared of snow by the tide and glistening clean in winter sunshine, he discovered two otters enjoying a meal. Coll and Coire were still devouring the big fish and were completely oblivious to any competition they might have. The breeze was blowing from sea to land, so no scent of fox alerted them. They continued their feast, blissfully unaware.

A long, lithe, rufous creature with a bushy tail was stealing from one vantage point to another along the edge of the wood, crouching low to the ground, creeping behind bog myrtle bushes, slinking round the back of boulders, pausing now and again in the shadow of a tree to check on his target, then patiently padding on again, ready to take all the time in the world in the catching of a worthwhile meal. In due course, he reached a large boulder in the tangle only

yards away from the youngsters – still unaware – and from which no
hint of his scent could carry to them. Suddenly, the sound of
chomping jaws was silenced, there was an explosion of fiery fur.
The red monster leapt and pounced, threw the two youngsters apart,
and grabbed their fish.

Coll and Coire, taken completely by surprise, recoiled growling
fiercely and hissing defiance. But, now, they could recognise that
strong scent. Fox! Normally each species tolerated the other but in
competition for much-needed food there could only be trouble. This
was a thief with whom they would not do battle! In only a moment,
Reynard was galloping away over the shore, a sizeable piece of
salmon in his jaws, and the young adults, not too upset, anyway, for
they had eaten their fill, sauntered up the bank of a nearby burn
which led to a convenient holt. Here, in the fastness of its
surrounding rocks, they would rest for a while. After a good clean-
up and quite unconcerned by their recent adventure, for it was all in
the day's work, they settled for a sleep.

Frog-marshing

At the mouth of a small highland river, where the tide came rolling in on a strong breeze, Coll and Coire found themselves in a strange situation never experienced before. Many a time they had trundled up little burns in the forest, sometimes to bathe in fresh water, sometimes just to check for small prey which might be caught and eaten. Sometimes, after heavy rainfall, these mountain streams turned into rip-roaring rapids on their way to the loch and these they had learned to avoid. But this was different. This wide expanse of restless water must be a very big burn, indeed! Actually, it was a river and the otter mother was leading her family through its turbulent waters. She was about to show them a part of their range they had never visited before.

It was hard work and tough after the long swim from Oakwood Bay, for they were battling upstream against waters rushing to meet the sea. Choppy waves slapped their faces as they paddled valiantly after their mother. They kept as close to her as possible and certainly did not observe the new kind of countryside on either river bank – flat lands stretching into the distance, dotted with small boulders and little pools. Had they but known it, they would later enjoy a splendid repast there.

In a little while, knowing her young ones were beginning to tire, Kelpie turned for one of the banks. As they scrambled ashore an indignant heron, fishing in a nearby pool, took off with an angry squawk and an outraged mallard mother hurried her family from the reeds into the river – they bobbed cheekily over the water to the other side. The cubs hardly noticed, so glad were they to be out of that chaotic waterway. They shook out their coats and began to potter about, sniffing for new scent. But their mother, with the usual command: *follow me*, was already setting off along a well worn track beside the river, so they hurried to catch up.

There was nothing particularly unusual about this path winding along the riverside, for there were many like it on the edge of the loch at home. It wandered in and out of sapling birches and small conifers growing sparsely on the bank, skirted round boulders too huge to scramble over, was lost in a small sandy bay but discovered again on the other side of it, and was bisected by several tiny trickling burns, each with a bed of small pebbles, which the cubs would have liked to explore. Their mother, however, kept urging them on and they, sensing a new adventure already, scurried to keep up. Reassuring was the scent of others of their kind filtering through the tangy smell of the sea. This must be an otter place!

The tumultuous stream still beside them, the family began travelling through a more wooded area and the pace slackened. Gnarled old trees, battered by many a storm and leaning away from the wind, were all around them, their stems clothed in soft, green lichens. Sunshine, through the swaying canopy above, dappled the moss-covered floor in gold. The path found a way through this pleasant place, in and out of the tall trees. Some of them grew right down to the water's edge, their roots straggling along the bank. Here were exciting holes and hollows for the cubs to explore. Progress became leisurely, an in-and-out of the water affair, as the youngsters followed each new intriguing scent and Kelpie seemed content that it should be so.

The otters made their way slowly upstream. Little by little, Coll and Coire became aware that the burn, once a white-capped monster roaring to the sea, had become a more gentle watercourse. Now it was chuckling happily along in a more sedate fashion and muzzles, exploring at the water's edge, found it no longer salt but as fresh as the burns at home. They came to a spot where it had split in two around a small, rocky island. On one side, it flowed swiftly onwards to the sea, but on the other the current was slow and turgid. A large pool with overhanging trees, dark and mysterious, had been created in the curving shelter of the bank. No restless water there.

It was beside this pool that Kelpie came to a sudden halt, so abruptly her cubs almost fell over her. What was this? They righted themselves and would have pressed past her motionless form in order to see what was happening, but the otter bitch growled softly and fiercely: *go back, be quiet.* So they froze into stillness and waited. Their mother seemed to be staring at something in the murky waters below, her whole attention fixed, nose twitching and eyes firmly focussed. The cubs could feel the tension and could hardly contain their excitement. Then, all at once, the adult was gathering herself for action, hindlegs preparing to spring. Anti-climax! Kelpie did not launch herself downwards, but hesitated instead, for the right moment. She lost her balance and Coll and Coire, taken by surprise, lost theirs too. There was an enormous splash as one, two, three – the whole family fell into the pool. As a large tidal wave began rolling away from the bank a salmon, streamlined and silvery, streaked from a secret place among the old tree roots and made all speed for the open sea.

After a good shaking out of their coats, the otter bitch and her cubs, unperturbed by this clumsy failure, continued on their way and, almost at once, were trotting through shallows over a wide pebble bed. Though the youngsters could not know it then, the salmon would come here to spawn when the time was right, and be easy to catch. For now, they found themselves quite at home in this new kind of burn, running in and out of the water, investigating scent along its banks, rough-and-tumbling in its welcoming coolness until a sharp whickering from their mother encouraged them on.

Very soon the cubs were aware of a strange rumbling sound in the distance, a kind of thunderstorm sound such as they were used to sometimes at home. But this was somehow different. Sensed but not recognised, it seemed to hold threat. However, their mother appeared to be unconcerned, so they kept close to her comforting presence and took no particular notice. Now they were passing through a more densely wooded area, the trees growing tall above their heads, their swaying tops bending in the breeze. It became rather gloomy and dark, and, trotting along behind their mother, the cubs were more and more curious as to where they were going and a little fearful, as well, because that ominous rumbling was becoming much louder.

The otter family rounded a long bend in the river's course. At once, the sound was overwhelming, blotting out the heartening chuckle of the water, the rustling of the leaves in the tees, the swish-swish of the surrounding vegetation as they padded through. A bewildering cacophony hit sensitive ears and frightened the small cubs out of their wits. And then, there it was, a gigantic wall of water falling from the rocky heights above, a deluge cascading down a cracked and creviced cliff face to the river below. The spray flew high to the top of the cliff and fell as gentle rain on the cowering cubs beneath. Sensing the force of that awful water, they turned to flee. But, once again, Kelpie reassured them: *it's all right, stay with me.* One day, she would show them the way round this frightening obstacle and it would lead them to a freshwater loch in the hills where brown trout might be caught. For now, she turned about and led them in among the trees.

A much-used deer path through the old trees by the river took them into a new kind of wood. It was not a bit like the wood in Oakwood Bay, at home, nor like the conifer forest which climbed to the ridges above Otter Cub Bay. These were much smaller trees, growing in long, straight rows, their branches bearing sharp needles which also covered the ground all about. Between each row was a deep 'ditch' which stretched into the distance and out of sight. It was along the bottom of one of these that their mother now led them and the sound of that fearful waterfall soon became a faint booming in the distance.

The ditches were full of new scents to follow up and wonderful places in which to play, as well. Soon the youngsters were running from one to the other, chasing each other up and down, in and out of the long furrows, rolling over and over in the abrasive needles on the bottom, kicking, biting, even pouncing disrespectfully on to the ample body of their mother. Free of fear, they could work off high spirits. A startled buck, suddenly disturbed, leapt right over their heads and galloped off to another part of the forest – the intrepid pair barely noticed. Echoing his indignant barking, a family of jays caught his alarm and flew from the treetops raucously scolding the cubs. They hardly heard this protest.

Gradually, the fine dry furrows began to be wet and muddy, with pools here and there and ferns growing on the dripping sides. Very quickly, low slung bodies were filthy, sleek coats matted, and webbed feet clogged. Accustomed to spending many minutes of each day drying off and cleaning up their pelts, the cubs began to feel uncomfortable and would have paused to groom. But their mother kept trotting on ahead, as if with some important purpose in mind and, of course, they must follow.

In fact, the otter family soon came to the end of the little trees and, all at once, found themselves in an even wetter place, a boggy marsh. Now they were padding over small islands of grass which sank beneath their feet into pools of muddy water, forging a way through thickets of reeds which reached far above their heads, and sometimes there was no vegetation at all – only a seemingly unending path of slimy mud. The cubs did not like this at all. Their coats became thickly plastered, their feet kept slipping and sliding in the greasy mire, and the scent was not one they liked at all. But their mother plodded on and instinct kept them close – without her they would surely be lost.

Miraculously, they came at last to the end of this horrible place and the marsh became the flat lands of the estuary. The pace quickened and, now, the otter bitch was leading her cubs on a pleasant track, in and out of little birches, over a carpet of short grass, and then to an area dotted all over with boulders large and small. Freshwater pools littered the ground and were inviting to the dirty and weary animals. All three dashed into the nearest one and in the usual turmoil of fun and frolic soon washed all the dirt away. But Kelpie had brought her family here for a special purpose – the timing was good, they were all hungry, and she was already picking up strong scent of the prey she knew would be there. Out on the springy grass again she hurried them on, nose to the ground, checking everywhere for whatever it was she was looking for. Puzzled, because they were hearing a ceaseless deep, grunting sound as well, Coll and Coire raced after their mother.

At last, she drew up beside a large pool and waited for her cubs to join her. A great 'croaking' filled the air and, in the water, a huge disturbance was taking place – splashings and bubblings all over the surface and a frenzied mass of 'things' the cubs had never seen before, heaving up and down, sinking down and bobbing up again. They were intrigued but not alarmed – the inviting scent had sent instant messages to hungry stomachs. Kelpie did not hesitate. She dashed into the water and began snatching, gobbling, and snatching again and, of course, they caught on at once. Soon the whole family was running from pool to pool, pouncing, scooping up the delicious morsels into wide open jaws, tossing them into the air, catching, chewing, swallowing, pouncing again. And the frogs were so busy with their mating, males fighting furiously with each other for females, the noise and confusion so great, that they were hardly aware of the predators among them. As for the otters, frogs were easy to catch and excellent eating, too.

Eventually, the greedy creatures could swallow no more. Hunger satisfied and feeling good, they cleaned up cheeks and chins, rolled a moment in the cool grass and, then, were ready to go. Lessons over for the moment, the otter bitch led her cubs over the flat lands of the estuary and back to the sea.

A Moment of Significance

Near the head of the loch, Kyle was crouched in the holt that he often used. He had recently caught and eaten a large eel, cleaned up his handsome fur coat and run up from the shore with sleep in mind. But in the confines of that nice, dry retreat he found himself restless, unable to settle, and kept changing position to curl his large body more comfortably. With no better luck. At last he gave up, stretched his limbs as well as he could in the cramped space, then crawled through the tunnel to its entrance. After carefully testing the air for alien scent, he came right out to take another look at his world of wild water, craggy rock and tangled seaweed.

It was early in May, the leaves on the nearby birch and rowan fresh green and fluttering bravely in a brisk breeze from the west. It rustled through a bank of heather and softly bent new fronds of fern. He watched it all idly not observing, of course, the beauties of nature but assessing their significance in whatever he might decide he was going to do. The loch was choppy. Small white horses chased each other over its surface to crash on the shore below. The sun was shining and he was warm in the shelter of the bank. There was no special hurry to do anything in particular, so he sat scratching his coat and had a roll in the bracken. He was just curling himself up for a nap, when, all of a sudden he froze. Abruptly, his head came up and scenting hard, whiskers twitching, ears and eyes alert, he was pointing towards the Narrows.

It was there, all right, lingering on the breeze, lost then picked up again, an inviting scent, a compelling message that required immediate action: *come, I am here*. In only a moment, he was racing

down the bank and charging over the shore to plunge into the restless waves. Diving, long and deep, deep and long, in a smooth, regular rhythm, he surfaced well out in the loch and was soon on his way through the Narrows. Impudent waves, slapping his face, meant nothing. A large eel skidding past did not tempt him. He had received an urgent call that must be instantly obeyed.

On Otter Point, Kelpie, poised on a tall, tangle-covered rock and totally absorbed, was waiting for a signal. Coll and Coire were asleep in the holt and not in her mind at all. A bull seal was storming through the Narrows, snorting loudly, rising high in the water to show off his impressive bulk and thrashing down again with a resounding smack, proclaiming to all his own species that the females in his harem were not for stealing. She noted his passing but was unimpressed. The spring tide was surging through the narrow channel, whirling and swirling as it always did, tide against wind. Living creatures of the sea were making use of this momentum to help them on their way, and inanimate objects, helpless, were inexorably sweeping along on unstoppable journeys to a faraway ocean. But, none of these things were of consequence to the otter bitch at this moment. She was waiting for the coming of her mate and though she would receive no warning on the wind, the tide might well bring his scent.

Kyle had heard no sound from his bitch, but on the breeze had come that unmistakable scent telling him: *I am ready. Come.* It was stronger each time he rose to the surface to breathe, speeding him on, telling him she was ready to mate. And, at last, Kelpie spotted him, a large otter swimming strongly towards the Point …Kyle! She whickered an excited welcome: *I am here,* then, in a great hurry to greet him, hurtled down over the rocks, clumsily leaping from one to the other, sliding out of control on the tangle, recovering at once to make again for the shore and only one instinct driving her. She needed her mate.

Kyle rose out of the water and scrambled ashore and, already, Kelpie was there to meet him. A great whickering of welcome filled the air and, at once, they were into the stimulating behaviour that would end in a mating. Kelpie led away over the playground of Otter Point, teasing the dog, enticing him: *catch-me-if-you-can,* and Kyle needed no encouragement. Straightaway, he was after her, chasing his provocative mate, nearly catching, almost catching, ready to nip if he did. But she was always just out of reach: *you can't catch me.*

Coll and Coire, hearing the sound but not understanding its significance, rushed out of the holt to join in the game. But their father, breaking away, repulsed the young dog with a nip to his nose and a growl: *this is my bitch, my place, get out,* and the young female, aware, now, of something unusual going on, retreated to the shelter of a nearby rock. Then both cubs were running for the safety of their holt. What was going on?

Kelpie led the way down over the rocks to the shore. Kyle hastened to follow. More excited whickering echoed around the Narrows and then the game continued, two amorous otters working up to a mating. The bitch slid into the water, rose high on a curling wave to call: *come on, come and catch me,* then dived. Now really roused, Kyle followed. As of one mind, they sailed side by side on the swiftly flowing waters, into Otter Cub Bay. Protected from the breeze by the buttress rocks at either end, it was calmer there and only tiny waves rippled ashore to stroke the weed. Here they continued the rumbustious wooing, sometimes over the slippery weed on the shore, sometimes playing hide-and-seek in the tangle of the shallows, the bitch twisting and turning away from her ardent mate and still not to be caught.

At last, both were ready. In the tranquil waters of the home bay, Kelpie, suddenly quiescent, now was waiting for her mate, drifting on the gentle tide, tapering tail held to one side, all invitation. Submission. Kyle glided alongside, grabbed her by the neck, covered her unresisting body with his and gripped her sides firmly with his paws. His thrusting loins completed the act and fierce growling from the bitch was evidence of his success. They were tied together for many a long moment.

In due course the pair broke apart. They raced for the shore and as if nothing special had been happening, sat companionably only a few feet apart, each shaking out its coat and grooming its luxurious fur. But this important event was not yet over. In only a little while, they were back in the water and had coupled again. The sheltered shores of Otter Cub Bay, with its fringe of birches bending in the

breeze and its fortress rocks at either end, provided a suitable background for the nuptials of Kyle and Kelpie.

And then, it was all over. In the days to come, they would mate again, but the initial deed was done. Kyle broke away, began swimming for the centre of the loch and a spell of foraging. Kelpie made her way back to the Point and her almost grown-up progeny. In due course, she would bring the next family of cubs into this otter world and begin, again, the business of teaching them how to survive. But for now, tired after all the excitement, she would sleep.

Towards Independence

Homo sapiens

A big holt, situated quite close to the Narrows, had room enough for Kelpie and her family, even though the cubs were now almost as large as she. It had been excavated beneath the giant rocks of an outcrop and was one that they frequently used when the nearby waters were too stormy or they needed to rest. It had two entrances, one a steep climb from the sea through a small gully, the other through a muddy tunnel which began as a dark hole in the wood behind. This wood was a rather wet one – lichen on the stems of the old oak trees, boggy places with clumps of yellow iris, and small boulders cushioned in moss, scattered all over the ground. It was a wonderful playground for the cubs. However, at this moment, the whole family was curled up in the holt, to sleep off a good meal.

But the day was hot. Three wet, warm bodies soon heated up and began to be uncomfortable. Coire could not settle. She became restless, needed to cool off, needed to stretch cramped limbs. She thought of the wood outside and the thought triggered action. With a big yawn and a brief glance towards her mother and brother, she eased away from their recumbent bodies and crawled into the tunnel. It was dark and damp in there with water dripping from the roof, but as she cautiously emerged, having first scented carefully for danger, she found herself in bright sunshine. Raindrops sparkled on the vegetation after a recent shower and the ground was patterned in darkest green and glittering gold. The little bitch sat herself down on a moss-draped rock and began to scratch her chin.

This was great. A nice breeze from the sea fluttered the leaves in the trees and lifted the fur on her sturdy, young body. She began to cool down and felt much more comfortable. She started to potter about her playground investigating its scents and stretching her cramped limbs. A small wood mouse felt the vibrations of her coming and scurried for its hole beneath the roots of a tree. Coire spotted it all right, but knowing there was no hope of catching, did not give chase. Two dung beetles struggled from beneath a heap of deer droppings and one fell over on to its back, waving its legs in the air until at last it rolled right way up again – she watched their antics, briefly, but as potential prey they were of no interest at the moment, so she left them alone. An old log, rotting on the green sward, drew her attention and she wandered over to take a look. With busy nose, she noted another creature there, not long ago – a fresh pile of droppings told her a roe deer had recently passed by.

But then, a big surprise! At the end of the narrow track, which passed through the wood and led onwards to the shore, something different, something which had never been there before had appeared. She halted at once and stood cautiously assessing. A tree? If it was, it had no branches or leaves all shivering in the breeze. A rock? Tall and thin and standing all alone, it did not look like any she had seen before. Most importantly, what scent did it have? The youngster lifted her head in order to catch whatever there was but the breeze did not help, for it was carrying any there might be past the outcrop and away up the loch. So, this 'thing' had no scent, and made no sound, either. Not alarmed and intensely curious, the young bitch remained motionless, staring, staring, and waiting for something to happen.

Out of the silence, a twig cracked suddenly. A tiny sound, but enough. Startled, Coire froze to the ground. The crisp report was not repeated and, receiving no alien scent and still curious, she waited to see what would happen. Then, the shock. Her eyes travelled higher on this peculiar new 'thing'. All of a sudden, short sighted eyes, more at home in dimmer conditions, connected with two strange, enormous eyes set in a round pale 'something'! Two pairs of eyes held, the one comprehending, the other not, and were locked together for a breathless moment. Instinct told the little otter to go.

Not really knowing why and not really frightened, she found herself padding back to her holt. With one backward glance at the strange 'tree' in her wood, she disappeared into its reassuring depths.

A delighted human being, smiling happily, continued on her way.

A marauder from on high

Coire was foraging in Duck Bay quite close to Otter Point. There was a holt there that she often used because she was mostly on her own these days, and it was one she had known well as a small cub. She was sensing change. Coll seemed more interested in exploring the waters and shores of the loch at the far end of their range, so they met only infrequently in brief, but friendly, encounters. Sometimes, as she foraged through the Narrows, she came across Torrie, Tangle's little bitch, and they would have an exuberant moment of greeting. Both young females found themselves solitary, with nothing much to do except forage for survival and keep clear of any territorially minded parents. One day, each might happen upon and play with new families of cubs on the loch and, one day, each might find herself a mate. There was no sign at all of Torrie's brother. Never far from Otter Cub Bay, Kelpie seemed occupied with other matters and their meetings were always short ones.

The cloud had hung low over the whole of the narrow loch for it had been raining since dawn and there was no wind to blow it away. But rays from the sun had begun to break through the overcast, splitting it apart, and turning all in that watery wilderness to gold. Coire was not one to note the beauties of nature, however. She was just fishing for a meal and had already caught and eaten an eel.

Another predator had not been so lucky. On an island, not too far away, where there were high cliffs and good nesting ledges, a pair of sea eagles had built their eyrie and the female was brooding her eggs. Her mate had lifted off to hunt for prey. Perched on a pinnacle of rock, high on the wooded hillside above Roedeer Bay, the male was waiting for a tiny movement, a quick glimpse of a fish in the water below. He had been there a long time for visibility had been poor and even eagle eyes had not been able to penetrate the gloom. But now, with sunshine shafting through the cloud, the light on the waters of the Narrows had improved.

Suddenly, those piercing eyes picked up a small stirring in the waters of Duck Bay – a tiny flurry of foam, then a small object moving over the surface, another stream of bubbles, then the small thing vanished from sight. It happened again. A fish? This raptor

111

had never caught an otter before, but this looked like prey. With no further delay, the huge bird lifted off its perch and began a long gliding flight from the heights, powerful wings spreading, closing a little, spreading again to maintain height, and rudder tail directing. In an instant, it was swooping low over Otter Point to land on a giant rock near the shore.

At that moment, Coire, completely unaware of the impressive predator from on high, surfaced quite close to the bird with a small fish in her jaws. The eagle spotted her at once, recognised fish, and lifting silently from its perch, swooped down to grab. But the swishing sound of air passing through wing feathers gave it away. Startled, the otter glanced up, realised instant disaster then, just in time, sank down into the seaweed forest of the shallows. The eagle, crashing into the water in a cloud of flying spray, missed both otter and fish, then rose with urgently flapping wings to fly back to its perch. Noting possible prey below, it would be prepared to watch and wait … for as long as was necessary.

The young bitch knew at once that the great bird would attack again. Diving as deep as was possible into the tangle, she set off to swim for a holt and safety. And, thus began a terrifying ordeal. Whenever she broke the surface to snatch a breath, that bird was there, plummeting down with feet outstretched, ready to grab. The tide was low, though beginning to creep in again, but because the water was so shallow, there was no safe hiding in the tangle. Her only course was to dodge in and around its waving fronds and to hope she could hoodwink the bird into thinking she was no longer there. What a hope! Her attacker had eagle eyes, eyes that could pinpoint the tiniest movement a long way off. Each time she rose to the surface, it was upon her. It was always there, hanging on broad wings with amazing control and ready to pounce with outstretched talons whenever a chance occurred. Each time she managed to dodge the attack with a twist and wriggle of her lithe body, but each time she was unable to fill her lungs with the air she needed so badly.

And otters must breathe. Her lungs were near to bursting and she was beginning to panic. Always her tormentor was overhead and following her every move. Then the worst moment yet. The dark eagle shape came swooping low across the bay, so low she did not see it coming. Suddenly, there came the terrifying rasp of its claws as they scraped through the fur on her neck. She froze, helpless in a moment of extreme fear. But eagle talons passed through a pelt wet and slippery and could not hold the unaccustomed prey. The youngster found herself sliding back into the water, free once again to try and escape.

Coire, now, was frightened out of her wits and with panic came realisation that she was tired and running out of energy. What could she do? Where could she go? There was no haven on the long, bare shores of Duck Bay, she knew that well, but as the slowly rising tide began to help her along, she suddenly realised she had arrived in familiar waters, comfortable waters that could take her to safety. Birchwood Point! There, she had often met with Tangle and her cubs. There were holts that could give her shelter. Instinct prompted her to make use of the tide, to use some of its energy, and to aim for the Point. With each hurried sinking into the tangle forest, she began to kick for home.

The persistent predator, however, was not ready to give up. Broad wings conferring total control enabled it to dip and dive over the water, plane low over its surface, swoop down to strike whenever its quarry came up for air, then rise, with little effort, to hover over her again. And, always, gimlet eyes spotted the little otter as she gasped for air. Instinct, combined with experience, told it the animal was tiring and with exhaustion would come submission and an end to the hunt.

But, miraculously, at last, Coire recognised the well-known shore to be close and the cavern holt, she had in mind, within reach. One last kick with weary hindlegs and she was there. No thought, now, to the hazardous journey from sea to holt. Helped ashore on a kindly, curving wave, she scrambled, slithered and slid over the slippery tangle as fast as tired legs would permit. Arrived at its dark entrance, she did not wait around to shake out her coat but straightaway vanished into its secure depths.

The eagle came sweeping low over the shore to land on a knife-edge of rock right above the holt. And there it perched, sharp eyes fixed on the entrance, poised ready to pounce whenever the animal reappeared. It waited a long, long time. Eventually, no otter prey emerging, it gave up and, still hungry, flew off for another part of the loch.

Rejection

Coire was crouched on the wide tangle shore of Duck Bay. She had caught a large lumpsucker and was now busy tearing it apart. A heavy mist hung low over the loch and provided kindly cover. No predatory creature had discovered her fish and she was able to continue her meal in a leisurely sort of way concerned, only, with filling her stomach. The merest whiff of a breeze, blowing up the loch, told her the tide had turned and was rising. Quite soon, there would be more fish.

In the deeper waters between Roedeer Bay and the seal skerries, Coll, with the stirrings of a hunger, was already looking for prey but with no success. He, too, noted the small breeze and with it that promise of fish arriving with the rising tide. Bored and needing a break, he decided to make for the skerries to see what was going on there. Perhaps he could catch a flounder in the sandy shallows which surrounded each one. The mist was starting to clear as he swam for the nearest rugged outcrop, and it was then that he discovered the seals. Seals! The enormous creatures, sprawling over every one of the rugged islets, appeared to occupy all the suitable spaces an otter might fancy for himself and were well-placed to launch themselves into the sea should he swim too close.

The young dog otter ignored them. Mostly, he knew, they would lie recumbent until the tide washed them off their smoothed and seaweed covered resting places, only raising lazy, languid heads to consider the world about them, or to shift their bodies into more comfortable positions. Instinct told him that with no small pups to protect, they would not be a threat to him. He began swimming slowly round each tiny island, searching for a vacant rock he could haul out on, and, eventually, needing rest and to groom his coat, climbed out beside a grey, mottled monster, too close for comfort. The seal raised a languorous head to assess the new arrival, but sank back, at once, unconcerned. Its eyes closed wearily, and the otter began a careful drying off and cleaning up.

Coll was just about to have a roll in the seaweed when, suddenly, he was all attention. A faint sound came wafting over the water, a plaintive, wistful calling: *where are you, let's meet.* Coire! The call came

115

again and hailed from somewhere in the Narrows. He slid back into the sea and began swimming as fast as he could for Otter Point.

The little bitch had been foraging in Duck Bay. She had caught a large eel, had taken it ashore to eat and now, no longer hungry, was back in the water. She would make for the nearest holt for a sleep. But then, she had picked up the scent of her sibling. It was faint on the incoming tide, but definitely there. Rather lonely, these days, for otters are sociable creatures within the family unit, and like to meet with each other when the opportunity occurs, she had responded at once with her excited summons.

Two otters were now swimming, as fast as they could, towards a meeting. Coll, leaving the skerries behind, swept along on the tide and with little effort found himself in the quiet waters of Otter Cub Bay. Coire, battling through the swirling waters of the Narrows, made for those same tranquil waters, that familiar safe place, for it seemed that his scent led her there. The two youngsters quickly realised each other's presence and swiftly came together. Rapturous greetings took place in a turmoil of turbulent water, a boisterous frolic of give and take wrestling, boxing and biting. The encounter was rougher than before, with an element of challenge in it, for these were young adults now, perhaps building to a time when each would defend territory and see off a competitor. The cacophony of their joyful whickering resounded all over the loch.

Kelpie heard the cheerful sound, too. It filtered through the graceful birches which fringed the shore and lifted through their fluttering leaves, unhindered, to the very top of the fortress rock. There, curled in a bed of dead bracken, a favourite coorie place of hers beside the old birthing holt, she had been awakened by the outrageous clamour. Pregnant, plump and in excellent condition, she knew, instinctively, that she must feed well before the birth of her family and would go foraging quite soon. But now, fully alert, she leapt to her feet and began running for the shore as fast as she could go.

Coll and Coire, still embroiled in their friendly engagement and quite unaware of an impending confrontation, came tumbling on to the tangle to continue the game. At the same moment, Kelpie arrived on the shore beside the little burn. She acted at once.

Growling angrily, she charged along the bank towards her impudent family and the cubs, delighted to discover their mother, tore towards her, whickering their pleasure, splashing great fountains of water into the air. There were no friendly greetings, however. The mother bitch ran at her cubs with bared teeth and hackles raised, all bristling pelt and bared teeth. Growling fiercely, she spat out a message that could not be ignored: *this is my place, get off, you are not wanted here.* The cubs recoiled in dismay, but as ever irrepressible, tried again, submissively creeping along the bank to be nearer to their mother and certainly not understanding her message. It came again: *this is my place, go.* She charged at them once more, and this time chased them back into the sea.

Coll and Coire, at first discomfited, went their separate ways, he to the waters far beyond Oakwood Bay, she to the holt on Otter Point. But they soon recovered from this surprising rebuff, evidently this was how it was to be now. This was normal. They must survive on their own.

A necessary adventure

It was early in the morning. A fiery red ball was rising in an angry sky above the faraway mountains, promising rough weather to come. It would be a suitable backdrop for a disturbing drama about to take place. Coll had been sleeping for a while in the Oakwood holt and had woken with a hunger that told him to go foraging. After crawling out of its confined quarters and giving his body a good stretching and scratching, he set off along a much-used track which would take him to the shore. Just as he was nearing the top of the outcrop above the bay, he picked up a scent he knew well. Kyle's. Straightaway, he began running to meet him, whickering his pleasure and hurrying to greet him.

He found his parent at the end of the track and received an unpleasant surprise. Ferocious growls and a snarling message were his welcome: *get off, this is my place, you are not welcome here!* The big dog otter came charging at his son, with hackles raised, bristling whiskers and bared teeth: *be off with you, go!* Taken aback by this rude reception, Coll was bewildered but, as yet, did not turn and flee. This was his parent! This was family! He whickered softly again, submissive, but still expecting acknowledgement. Then Kyle flew angrily at the young male, giving him a nasty bite on the nose and tearing one of his ears. That was enough. The dismayed animal turned around, and fled. He hurled himself down the rough rock route to the sea, and was soon making his escape across Oakwood Bay. Kyle did not give chase.

Coll soon recovered. Another lesson had been learned – this parent, like his mother, no longer wanted him around. The salt water stung his wounds but he hardly noticed. Hunger, and the recent encounter, drove him onwards, swimming fast, diving shallow, first making sure of escape from an angry father then looking for a meal. Eventually, forced to rest a while, he paused to look around and to note any significant scent in the air. All of a sudden, it dawned on the inexperienced youngster that the loch had become very large indeed, in fact so large there was no familiar scent of a shore close at hand and no instinct that there might be one, either. This was different. This was frightening.

119

The young dog swam aimlessly round in small circles wondering what to do next. Then, taking him by surprise, right below in the deep clear water a large silvery salmon flipped by. Hunger and the need to hunt defeated alarm. With a quick arching of his body, he was diving into the depths to streak after the tempting creature. Fish! Food! Coll was once again into a familiar routine and fear was forgotten. He lost the salmon to superior speed but soon discovered that fine fish were here in plenty, in this huge expanse of the loch. Very soon, he spotted his favourite prey, a large eel making its way up the loch, and was after it, at once. After a long chase and several attempts to grab it, his supple body matching every action of the elusive creature, he had a slippery, wriggling fish in his jaws that was determined to escape. It would not be subdued and, certainly, it could not be eaten in the water.

Frantically, Coll looked around the unfamiliar seascape for a landing – he had no intention of dropping his prize. It was in this moment of panic that the young adult became aware, for the first time, of a shore some distance away. All this time, the tide had been taking him in its direction and, now, a distant haven, it seemed he must attempt to reach it. Kicking hard with all his might and with his head pulled to one side with the weight of the creature, he battled gamely towards a new shore and a good meal. In due course, triumphant and almost exhausted, he dragged his still squirming prey on to a thick carpet of seaweed beneath a wheeling, whirling storm of gulls screaming hate at him from above.

Coll ignored the gulls. He shook out his coat, paused a moment to catch his breath, then noting the eel making a determined effort to return to the sea, secured it with a lightening paw. Wasting no more time, he began eating the best fish he had ever caught to an accompaniment of protesting birds – they were of no consequence to him and it was only a little later that he discovered their nests and gobbled an egg or two. Satisfied, at last, the youngster began looking around to discover where he was and if this was a safe place for an otter to be. He noted the scent of his species, not strong, but coming to him from every direction. Certainly, an otter place. After a token cleaning-up of his cheeks and chin, he set off to explore.

Scenting busily all the while, the eager animal left the moist tangle behind and found himself stumbling over an uneven shore of broken rock draped in old and dried up seaweed. It cracked and crunched beneath his feet. He trotted across an area of grass, spring green and already well-cropped – a pile of deer droppings told him what animal had been there. He threaded a way through patches of bog myrtle, narrow and secret paths but well-defined and the scent was so strong it masked all others. Then he was passing through thick, bushy heather which brushed his coat as he passed – already it had a hint of summer fragrance. On the far side of the heather bed, a decision had to be made.

A track led off in two directions, one on either side of him. Both were well-trodden and otter scent was stronger than ever. He paused to consider. What if he met with one? After the recent experiences with each of his parents and his nose still sore, he was not too sure. Nevertheless, the urge to investigate was strong – this seemed a good place to be and perhaps he would stay for a while. Turning into a strengthening breeze, the young male began slowly to traverse one of the paths, taking his time, poking his nose into this and that, all the while on the look-out for trouble and ready to flee for the sea, if necessary. It wandered through heather, rough and spiky, meandered round prickly bushes of gorse, disappeared beneath a crackling of bracken, and continued on, and on.

Then Coll was hesitating beside a grass hummock, his nose testing busily. A dark dropping had been deposited on the top and it smelled of fish and was full of tiny pieces of bone. Definitely an otter message! Up-tail and squatting, he left one of his own. As he padded along over the well-used path, he became more and more confident. All the right signs were there: dark droppings at intervals along the path, patches of salt-blackened soil where prey had been torn apart and eaten, torn scraps of decaying fish and the tattered tough skin of a dogfish, the discarded shells of crab and mussel scattered everywhere, even a coorie place in the bracken where an otter had recently been lying. Then, as it were to set the seal, he came upon a small holt beneath a sheltering slab of rock, right above a smooth granite face sweeping down to the sea. A small willow bush grew beside it and there were footprints in damp soil, as well. Though his nose told him this secret holt was vacant, he quickly passed by, just in case.

It was when the young explorer came to a halt on a patch of grass, and was giving his coat a good scratching that he suddenly noticed something most peculiar. He had been here before! Down below was the spread of broken rock and dead seaweed over which he had climbed from the sea. Behind was the track he had been exploring. In front, the one upon which he had set out. He was sure of it – he could smell his own scent. This was where he had started this exciting adventure and he could go no further. The youngster did not realise it, of course, but he had just experienced his first island. He looked around, bewildered. Short-sighted eyes noted the sea from which he had come with his eel – flurries of foam in the stiffening breeze, no sunshine, but an infinity of grey, restless water. There was plenty of space out there! Instinct took him down to the water's edge. He would swim along this peculiar shore and see where it led.

Coll paddled slowly round the little island, bouncing on the waves, nosing through them when they rolled past too tall, pausing from time to time to scent and look all around and floating feet up, for a rest, when he arrived in more sheltered water. A small headland loomed ahead and he made a strange discovery. At the one moment, the tide had been slowly and gently carrying him along, the next, as he rounded those gigantic rocks, it had suddenly become a relentless force to battle against – an element of island foraging that he would soon become accustomed to. Now, of course, he was realising that in this new place, there were no long shores of the tangle along which to forage, and no sheltered bays, each with its fortress rocks to guard it. Indeed, it was remarkably like one of the skerries at home, only larger – an outcrop of rock surrounded by the sea. On an archipelago of small islets, he now observed a group of those seals watching him go by. Finally, by now extremely tired and there being no other place near to make for, he coasted ashore in the remembered rhythm of the waves, dropped a spraint message on the tangle: *I am here*, then, reckoning this place to be safe, ran to a coorie spot in the heather.

Coll would soon discover that this small island in the loch was where he would meet with young otters from other ranges, where he could exist without serious challenge. Though occasionally visiting the home loch, he would spend much of his time in this area. Here were no breeding holts to be defended. Here, young sub-adults, no longer welcome in their parents' territories, could find temporary shelter and social exchange with one another, and a plentiful supply of fish in its waters. It was a safe place. In due course, if they survived to become adult, each youngster would have to look for a vacant territory elsewhere, and a mate.

An end and a beginning

In its wilderness of craggy hillsides, the loch of the otters, serene and untroubled, was mirrored in an azure sky. It was midsummer. Small islands, dotted here and there in the outer loch, were emeralds in a tapestry of blue. Tangled rock shores shimmered in warm sunshine, kaleidoscopes of ever-changing brown, green, orange and yellow, and rugged outcrops, brooding over each roughly scalloped bay, were ancient rocks seemingly there for ever. Oak, ash, birch and holly patchworked the hillsides in variegated green, and dark conifer trees, relieved by verdant larch, climbed to the broken ridges above. They enfolded this enchanting place in lonely magnificence and its wild inhabitants all went undisturbed about their business, the business of survival.

A fox trod delicately over the seaweed in Duck Bay. During the night he had stalked and killed a sickly deer calf and with difficulty had carried it to his vixen on the hill. Five growing cubs she had in her den, and they were always hungry. He was ravenous, now, and was hunting for himself, each clump of glistening seaweed investigated by his efficient nose, its slippery strands scraped aside for a lurking crab beneath. Nearer Otter Cub Bay, five red deer hinds and a young stag were making leisurely progress to the hill, sauntering over the close cropped grass, sniffing here, nibbling there, pausing now and again to chew and look around. From the nearby skerries, the seals watched their passing indifferently, dozing away the time until the rising tide would wash them afloat. A pair of golden eagles, chicks well-fed and safe on their eyrie, soared and stooped in the heavens above, free for a moment from parental care.

In the Narrows, Kyle, the dominant dog otter, was serenely sailing through on his back, the waters placid and the tide moving him along. He was looking for interlopers in his territory. Suddenly alert, he rolled right way up and began scenting hard. There was a stranger in Otter Cub Bay! Kelpie would be in her holt! He followed his nose into its sheltered waters and paddled slowly along the shore. Nothing there. He climbed the steep gully of the fortress rock. Looking down into the next little bay, he once again discovered an intruder, a young male who had no business to be there. Whickering an unmistakable message: *get out of here,* Kyle tore down over the rocks to chase him into the loch then, completely unruffled, resumed his leisurely patrolling along the shore. It was all just routine.

Coire, a young adult now and beautiful as her mother, was foraging in Roedeer Bay. She had just caught a large eel and, after a struggle with the frantically wriggling creature, was making for dry land. A shallow dive into the tangle and then she was rolling ashore in a commotion of foaming water, her fish still safe. A sharp bark of alarm, then another and another, was her greeting. A roe buck, nearby, nibbling on juicy tendrils of seaweed, was taken completely by surprise. But the otter was a creature he knew well so, knowing his doe was quite safe, he returned happily to his meal. She had her young fawn close beside her and was browsing in the wood. Unperturbed by this noisy objection, Coire began to tear her succulent prey apart. And so, they continued peacefully together, the roe deer and the otter, in perfect harmony on the glistening weed.

In a little while, the buck sauntered off into the trees to join his family, but Coire was not alone for long. Two hoodie crows came flying softly and speculatively over her head, then alighted on a rock only a small distance away. With beady eyes they considered the fish at her feet. An easy meal? But the youngster, grown-up now and experienced in the ways of these predators, just kept a watchful eye on them and was ready to defend her prize if necessary. In due course, they flew away still hungry, and the young bitch finished off her meal. A long time was spent in grooming her coat in the sunshine, parting the matted fur on chin and chest and smoothing it back into place, then she trotted back into the loch.

Kyle had arrived in the deeper waters around the seal skerries. Here were fish to be caught, so he paused in his patrolling to forage for a meal. It was while he was lying on his back enjoying a small eel that, all of a sudden, he picked up the scent of another otter. Dropping his prey, at once, he quickly changed course and began swimming as fast as he could for Roedeer Bay. Very soon, he recognised the scent of one of his cubs and also, automatically, that this was a young female not in season, not yet ready to mate. Coire, of course, knew her father. Whickering noisily, the two came together and were immediately into a carefree greetings game that proclaimed to the rest of the otter world that they were there and happy to meet. But, as usual, nowadays, it was only a short encounter. The big male had other matters on his mind. All of a sudden, he was swimming for the next big outcrop along the shore and the young female, tired now and with a full stomach, was making her way towards the mouth of a small burn. She had in mind a secret holt on one of its banks. She would sleep for a while.

Just as Kyle was leaving Roedeer Bay, Coll was running over the rocks in Oakwood Bay. He seldom risked being in the sheltered waters of the home loch, nowadays, but had found himself there after a lengthy chase after a fish. No other otters around, he had crawled into one of the holts in the wood. Now, after a good sleep, he was returning to the water and would make for that island he had recently discovered. But, as he breasted into water rippling on a small breeze in the bright sunshine, he suddenly picked up an unmistakable scent. Kyle! There was no friendly whickering from the big dog otter as he came swimming to see off his son, and the young male did not wait around to attempt a greeting. Diving deep and long, he swam as fast as he could for the safety of the outer loch and Kyle, his duty done, returned to Oakwood Bay. There he would wait for the tide to turn and an easy patrolling to the head of the loch.

On a soaring to the surface for a much-needed breath, Coll discovered himself close to his island. More and more, it seemed a good place to be and he often went ashore there with prey to eat, to groom and to snatch a short sleep. Each time there was fresh spraint on the winding track which circled the island, but it was spraint that held no warning or threat and was certainly not his father's. Sooner or later he would surely meet with these otters and find them friendly. Now, hungry again after all that exercise, he began to forage and would take his fish on to the rocks, to eat.

Then, the dilemma. He had caught a large eel after a long chase, but suddenly realised the island had vanished. The tide had long since carried him past and it was nowhere to be seen. Where could he take his fish? Ahead he could see nothing but shimmering waters with no welcoming shores beyond. He would have to let go of his hard won prize. But, just in the nick of time, there came a small breeze wafting scent on the air. It was scent that he recognised, seaweed scent! Safe landfall must be in that direction. Slowly, laboriously, he began to swim into the wind, hauling his lively fish along in his jaws, hanging on to it for dear life. The scents grew ever stronger, both seaweed and woodland smells, and eventually, greatly relieved and almost exhausted, he was able to dive through a tangle fringe, to bring his prey on to a shore where he had never been before. He shook out his coat, scented briefly for possible competition, then got down to business.

It was while Coll was busy tearing and chewing, totally absorbed in the process of enjoying a good meal, that he became conscious of a strange rumbling sound from somewhere nearby. Startled, he raised his head to listen and look. This, he had never heard before. The 'thing', whatever it was, came nearer and nearer, roared a warning, then passed away, its alien sound fading into the distance and becoming nothing. Reassured, the young adult resumed his feast. But a short time later the sound was repeated, louder this time and seeming to vibrate through every nerve in his body. It became a deafening, thundering, overwhelming sound so that he almost panicked, turned tail and fled for the sea. But, once again, it rumbled onwards and away, then could not be heard at all. And, it kept on happening at irregular intervals until, at last, the young otter hardly noticed it at all, the most important aim in life to consume his fish.

When he could eat no more, Coll began to clean-up his coat, wiping cheeks and chin along the moist tendrils of the tangle to remove all traces of his meal. He rolled in the weed, rubbed throat, breast and stomach over the luxurious carpet, then scratched and nibbled at his fur to smooth it back into place. At last satisfied, he stood poised a moment watching the sea, a fully-grown male, resplendent in lustrous brown coat and muscles that rippled along his back. He was comfortable inside. He was ready to go. Now he would start exploring this new place and this would continue the process by which, eventually, he would find territory not held by another dominant male, one which he could claim as his own, and in which, in due course, he would found a family.

It was only a short distance from the tangle to a border of grass and then he was climbing a steep bank densely covered in scattered boulders and bracken. No otter scent there, no tracks of any other animal. But... what was this? Before him, there was a strange 'something' he had never seen before. It stretched out of sight on either side of him and was dark and mysterious, giving him no clue as to what it might be. An inquisitive nose discovered an alien scent. A cautious paw found it hard and perhaps safe to venture on to. He hesitated, unsure what to do. But over on the other side of this 'thing' he could scent and see a wood. In its shelter he would surely find cover and perhaps a spot where he could rest. Cautiously trying out the peculiar substance a final time, he made up his mind to cross over.

It was a fatal decision. Coll was trundling happily across the highway when, without warning, there came again that rumbling sound. Almost at once, it became a ghastly fortissimo, assaulting his sensitive ears, blotting out all understanding and instinct, building to a thundering, roaring, cataclysmic monster. Rubber screamed on tarmac. A human being swore. And, on the dark, unyielding highway, a broken otter body twitched a time or two, then was still. Coll was dead. Coll was no more.

. . . .

On the fortress rock, above Otter Cub Bay, cascading strands of ivy curtained the entrance to the birthing holt. Soft shafts from the early sun filtered through to reveal the cracked and creviced rocks within. Tucked away in its furthest shadowed recess, on a bed of dead grass and leaf litter, two tiny cubs lay with their mother. Helpless and feebly kicking, they were enfolded in the protective curve of her long, lean body. Sound was the brisk rasping of her tongue as she cleaned them up, the soughing of the sea from far below, and the drip-drip-plop of falling water into a small pool outside. Kelpie knew nothing of the premature death of one of her cubs, but she had just given birth to a new family, the beginning, once again, of that long process of care and attention which would ensure the continued survival of her species. A new Coll and Coire had arrived in the otter world.

Lutra lutra

O tters are members of the weasel family, *Mustelidae*, carnivores who are remarkable for their long bodies and short legs. Within this family are weasels, stoats, martens, polecats, mink (*Mustelinae*) and otters (*Lutrinae*). Many people are of the belief that the otters they see along our rocky coastlines and in our many sea lochs are sea otters. This is not the case. *Enhydra lutris is* only found on the west coast of North America and along the more remote shores of Japan and North East Asia. Our otters, whether they have their being in our rivers, freshwater lochs, or in coastal areas are all of the same species *Lutra lutra*, the Eurasian otter. They used to be found, in suitable habitat, almost anywhere from Ireland to Japan, from Arctic Finland to North Africa and even as far south as Indonesia.

Lutra lutra has vanished from many areas for various reasons, pollution of its environment, disappearance of suitable breeding sites, and persecution probably being the most significant. Nowadays, in Britain, otters survive in reasonable numbers on the rocky coasts of the West Highlands of Scotland, the Western Isles and Shetland, Northern Ireland and, to a lesser extent, in Wales, Devon and Cornwall. However, the cleaning-up of rivers and freshwater lakes in many places is encouraging the return of the animal to these areas in small numbers.

The otter spends a great deal of its life in water, for that is where it hunts for its food, mainly fish. It has, therefore, evolved to survive in that habitat. Its pelage is thick and waterproof. The head is rather flat, offering little resistance to the water when swimming. Webbed feet, powerful haunches and rudder-like tail enable the animal to move at speed when hunting prey and once caught, well-developed claws and sharp teeth help to hold it and devour it. Sight is probably not particularly good on land, but scenting powers and hearing are extremely sensitive. In the water, in especially murky conditions, the whiskers (vibrissae) pick up vibrations from its quarry and help in locating its movements. The ears and nose are automatically closed in the water. The animals are on average over a metre in length, the males weighing around 10kg, the females 7kg.

In the past, the otter was much hunted for its fur or just for so-called sport. Since 1981 it has had the protection of the Wildlife and Countryside Act which prohibits its killing anywhere in Britain.